EMBRACING LIFE'S JOURNEY

An Exploration of Wisdom, Growth & Resilience

John R. Schneider

ISBN: 979-8-218-98897-5

© 2024 by John R. Schneider
Original Artwork by CreateAVision Media
Cover & Contents Designed by Gordon Bond
Edited by Donna Speranza
Printed in the United States of America

All rights reserved. No part of this book may be reproduced, distributed, or transmitted in any form or by any means, including photocopying, recording, or other electronic or mechanical methods, without the prior written permission of the publisher, except in the case of brief quotations embodied in critical reviews and specific other noncommercial uses permitted by copyright law. For permission requests, visit CreateAVisionMedia.com.

This book offers general information and insights based on the author's personal experiences and reflections. It is not a substitute for professional advice, diagnosis, or treatment. Readers should seek the advice of qualified healthcare providers or other professionals regarding personal health, mental well-being, or other issues. The author and publisher are not liable for any actions taken or not taken based on the contents of this book. Any application of the ideas, practices, or techniques shared in these pages is done at the reader's discretion and responsibility. Always consult a qualified professional before making significant life changes, particularly in health, relationships, or finance.

Note on Images:
Most of the images in this book are original, somewhat abstract, and without captions. Hopefully, this blend of text and visuals creates an intellectually stimulating and artistically engaging book.

Dedicated to My Daughter, Jeanne...

...for the joy you bring into my life, this book is for you in gratitude for all you are now and all you continue to become. I am proud of you. Always remember to take the time to appreciate your beautiful journey through life.

— Love, Dad

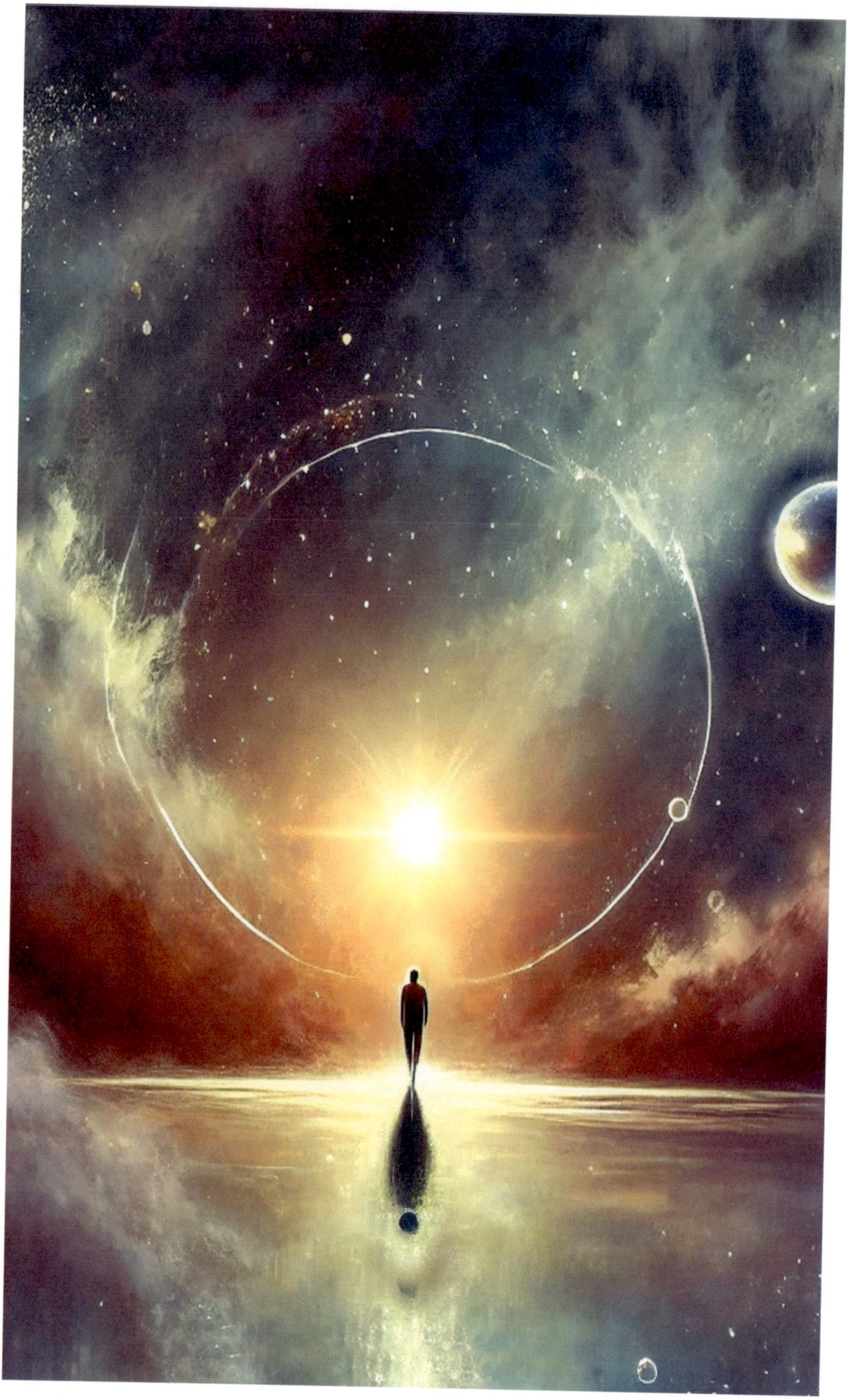

Thoughts from the Editor

Throughout this book, John Schneider explores life's complex, beautiful, and often challenging journey through various lenses—personal experiences, philosophical insights, and emotional reflections. He delves into wisdom, the importance of resilience, the power of humor, and the acceptance of life's impermanence.

From navigating life's obstacles to embracing disintegration, from cultivating true wisdom to visualizing a better future, the themes of growth, transformation, and personal evolution are central to the book he has written for all of us.

He begins by examining the nature of wisdom and how it often emerges through life's most challenging moments. He looks at how intuition, rationalization, and the balance of internal voices guide us and the profound ways that humor can lighten our burdens. He ventures into understanding relationships, the power of positive thinking, and the art of letting go when things fall apart—whether it's our bodies, our careers, or our identities.

At the heart of this exploration is the notion that life is an ongoing journey. We are constantly learning, evolving, and adapting. While we may never reach perfection, pursuing growth and self-awareness is the key to a fulfilling life. Whether through humor, resilience, or wisdom, we are always moving forward, becoming more attuned to ourselves and the world around us.

As John has told me quite often, life is about embracing the process, not reaching a destination. The wisdom we gain, the humor we find, the resilience we build, and the lessons we learn shape us. I know he truly hopes that the reflections and insights in this book serve as reminders to approach life with openness and curiosity.

John's book will undoubtedly make us think seriously. It may also make us smile just a little as we recognize the absurdity of life and realize that we are all part of a cosmic comedy. Life can be challenging, yes—but it's also filled with moments of joy, wonder, and unexpected humor. Through my trials and tribulations, and from John, I've learned that we can face whatever comes with grace and a sense of peace by holding on to that lightness.

On a personal note, my journey has also been shaped by resilience and transformation, much like the themes explored in this book. As someone deeply involved with Alcoholics Anonymous, I've had the privilege of walking alongside people as they navigate the toughest challenges in their lives. As a humble member of AA, I've seen firsthand the power of community, the strength that comes from vulnerability, and the immense capacity for growth in all of us.

Being part of AA has taught me that transformation is always possible, even in the darkest moments. It's about showing up for yourself and facing life's obstacles with honesty and courage, knowing that you don't have to do it alone. These messages are conveyed throughout this book—lessons about resilience, growth, and the importance of embracing life in all its messy, beautiful impermanence.

We don't have all the answers, and maybe we never will. But I know the journey is rich for John, and there's beauty in the questions and the unknown. Life for him has been a constant dance between holding on and letting go, striving and surrendering, thinking and feeling. Embrace that dance, and trust that your path—wherever it may lead—has meaning, purpose, and rhythm.

Thank you for allowing me to be a part of this process.

— Donna Speranza

Acknowledgment

    I am deeply grateful to the friends, family, and colleagues who have been part of my journey and the philosophers, historians, and authors whose ideas have sparked my reflections—special thanks to fellow author Michael T. Houghton and to Gary Deverman, who have been lifelong friends. While many of the ideas in this book are uniquely mine, most are built on the wisdom of others and reimagined to align with my unique understanding of life's journey. This book is my way of sharing those reflections with you in the hope that they may offer something of value.

— John Schneider

"I think books are like people, in the sense that they'll turn up in your life when you most need them."

— Emma Thompson

Contents

Preface .... **i**

1 - Birth as a Symphony **1**
Imagine life's beginning as a metaphorical symphony, blending chaos, rhythm, and harmony to set the tone for existence.

2 - Positive Pain & Building Resilience **11**
Early pain and struggle shape our growth, encouraging resilience and viewing challenges as transformative.

3 - The Relativity of Life: Einstein's Insights **19**
Our perception of time and space influences our life's journey.

4 - Time & Space Conundrum **29**
Balancing the present moment with our physical world impacts our choices and significant life events.

5 - Spiritual Faith & Inner Guidance **37**
The role of belief, whether traditional or personal, guides us through life's uncertainties.

6 - Stimulating Senses & Emotional Awareness **45**
Our senses and intangible perceptions enhance our awareness of the world.

7 - Judging, Evaluating & Letting Go **53**
Freeing ourselves from constant judgment allows us to live more authentically.

8 - Harnessing Intuitive Rationalization **61**
Trusting instincts in decision-making while balancing rational thought helps us balance everything we need to move forward.

9 - Echoes of Forgiveness **71**
The transformative nature of forgiveness brings freedom to live life more fully

10 - Sexual Dynamics & Power 79
The role of sexuality in control, manipulation, and relationships is worth understanding.

11 - Women & Men in Shared Spaces.. 85
It's always important to navigate gender dynamics with mutual respect and understanding.

12 - Embracing Solitude for Inner Peace 93
The value of solitude is in fostering self-reflection and resilience.

13 - Acceptance: It Is What It Is 101
Releasing the need to control or change reality helps create a more peaceful life

14 - The Power of Humor 109
Using humor as a powerful tool can help navigate life's challenges.

15 - Dance of Control & Surrender 117
Balancing control means letting go and embracing uncertainty.

16 - Moving Through Obstacles 125
Leveraging patience and wisdom helps us move through life's challenges.

17 - Identity in Flux 131
Embracing the fluid nature of identity happens during different phases of life.

18 - The Paradox of Purpose 139
Navigating the complexities of finding purpose and meaning takes time.

19 - Harnessing the Mind 147
Exploring the power of visualization, positive thinking, and the emergence of wisdom can create new opportunities.

20 - Embracing Resilience & Crafting a Legacy.................... 157
Turning personal loss and internal struggles into growth is necessary.

21 - Disintegration & Transformation 161
Accepting life's impermanence and renewal cycles is part of personal growth.

22 - Tsunami of Memories 169
Reflecting on the role of memories and the life review helps shape our final moments.

23 - Un-finishing Your Life 175
Embrace life as an ongoing, open-ended journey, focusing on growth rather than closure.

24 - Personal Affirmation 183
Using affirmational reflections to realign with core lessons and values.

25 - Just One More Thing.. 189
We should always ask questions even when they may never be answered.

Appendix & Glossary of Concepts... 197

Bibliography & Suggested Reading 200

About the Author 205

Embracing Life's Journey

Preface

"The important thing is this: to be able at any moment to sacrifice who we are for what we might become."
—*Charles Du Bos*

This quote from Charles Du Bos (left, 1882–1939), a French literary critic, captures the essence of transformation, growth, and the courage to embrace change. It reflects the themes I've experienced in my life and what I explore in this book.

The word "sacrifice" here means more than just letting go of what's comfortable or uncomfortable; it's about relinquishing parts of ourselves—habits, beliefs, even relationships—that no longer serve us to make space for who we might become.

Personal evolution isn't a linear process toward a destination. Instead, life is an ongoing transformation journey, with each stage inviting us to release what's outdated and embrace what's next. Du Bos reminds us to be open to uncertainty, as it's in the unknown that actual growth occurs.

The most incredible transformations often come when we release outdated versions of ourselves and embrace what's next, even if it's uncertain. Growth takes courage and a willingness to let go of security for the sake of possibility.

I've shared this philosophy of evolution with my daughter, Jeanne. Her journey has taught me as much as I have shared with her. Watching her grow into a robust and resilient person has been a constant reminder of transformation's power. Recently, Jeanne honored me by getting a tattoo of a symbol embodying the philosophy I shared with her while she was growing up.

Again, this book is dedicated to her. It reflects everything we've learned about resilience, courage, and embracing change. I hope we all continue to trust our instincts, follow our hearts, and learn from our experiences. We cannot ask much more than that from our lives.

This book didn't start with a grand mission to enlighten the world. It began as a reflection on the twists, turns, and lessons that life has thrown me. Somewhere between the laughs, the insights, and the curious stories, I realized that my experiences weren't just for my amusement; they held something worth sharing. So, here I am, offering up my perspectives, stories, and insights in a way I hope will be entertaining and meaningful.

You don't have to read this book from start to finish to find something valuable. You're already on your journey, wherever you are today or wherever you'll be tomorrow. The real question is—are you embracing it fully? It's a question I ask myself, too.

This book celebrates life's mysteries and offers insights on embracing the journey more deeply. Enjoy the read wherever it may take you.

A word of caution, however. Many of us turn to self-help books for guidance through life's complexities. I once had a library full of them. While these books can inspire, they sometimes offer one-size-fits-all solutions that oversimplify complex issues, promoting unrealistic expectations of instant change. Fundamental transformation requires time, patience, and perseverance.

Preface

This book invites you to take a thoughtful, reflective approach to growth rather than a shortcut. Try not to search for answers here, but instead, let yourself find the warm glow of inspiration to support you in your own journey.

Some individuals write self-help books without credentials in psychology or counseling, and this one is no exception. You caught me. Still, I hope this book will feel like a supportive companion on your journey. I intend my insights to spark thought, not prescribe a specific path.

I encourage you to reflect on, adapt, or even reject ideas based on your experiences. Actual growth doesn't come from following a rigid formula but from shaping insights that resonate with your life. No magic words enable anyone to transform themselves merely by reading. Sorry.

I recognize that, for many, chronic pain, severe mental anguish, or physical limitations can shape every aspect of life, often placing unique constraints on what is achievable or fulfilling. While this book explores general themes of resilience, transformation, and growth, these concepts are not intended to diminish the reality of living with chronic pain or a physical disability. Instead, I hope you can adapt the ideas here to fit your experience. My goal is to provide perspectives, tools, or insights that honor your journey as it is, not as anyone thinks it 'should' be.

As you read, consider the balance between hope and caution in your decision-making and how experience can guide you through different circumstances. I hope those navigating life's complexities will find something valuable here. Trust your instincts, listen to your heart, and embrace life's wisdom.

Enjoy Your Journey!

— *John Schneider*

Preface

"Just as a compass aligns with Earth's magnetic field, our intuition aligns us with our true purpose."
– *Unknown Source*

Embracing Life's Journey

From the first breath, life erupts like a symphony—a burst of sound and sensation woven into the silent, waiting air. The rhythms of existence pulse in time with the heart's first beats, and a world unfolds, chaotic yet choreographed, like notes scattered across a page, only to find their harmony in motion. Life's symphony swells, each moment a movement, every heartbeat a drum keeping time with the cosmos.

Chapter 1: Birth as a Symphony

In the Beginning…

Before birth, I was a life form of some kind within my mother—a drifting entity not fully awake in the conscious world. I remember pieces of the experience in small, scattered fragments like scenes from a dream. These remnants of our embryonic journeys are tucked away in our ancient memories. They linger quietly, reminders of that mysterious, unfiltered world we once inhabited, gently guiding us from within as our most basic primitive human instinct.

Then comes the moment we're ready to be born. Together with our mothers, we work to emerge into the light, catching faint glimmers in the distance—like a misty vision of the future taking form around us. Suddenly, we're propelled into our new existence with almost jarring intensity. Hooray. We arrive for the first time in a foreign but oddly familiar world. For me, it sometimes feels like it happened yesterday. At other times, the experience seems long past.

I didn't know it at the time. Still, my first experience of separation when leaving the womb and entering the unknown world set the stage for all that followed—a subtle, enduring reminder of both the beauty and the ache of beginning anew.

Because my parents were divorced before I was born, my mother was a bit gloomy, and a nest of baby bluebirds in a tree right outside her hospital window cheered her up. She remembered a specific moment when she was thinking about how challenged we'd both be without a husband or a father.

Later, my mother told me that a popular song in 1949 had cheered her on. The song was "Accentuate the Positive" by Johnny Mercer. Its upbeat message encouraged everyone to focus on the good, let go of negativity, and embrace a positive outlook on life. I probably have that musical memory inside me, as well. Music has always been a part of my life.

There is a line in William Shakespeare's play, *Twelfth Night*, that says, "If music be the food of love, play on." I was an actor who spoke that line in that play, and I'll never forget it. Music sustains and enriches the human spirit and has done so for me throughout my life. I always felt so uplifted when listening to recorded or live music. Bob Marley, one of my favorite musicians, famously said, "One good thing about music is that when it hits you, you feel no pain." This lyric from his song "Trenchtown Rock" reflects Marley's deep belief in music's ability to uplift and heal, particularly in the face of hardship and struggle.

Then there's Leonard Bernstein, who said: "Life without music is unthinkable. Music without life is academic. That is why my contact with music is a total embrace."

Bernstein's words resonate deeply with me. They remind us of life, like music, as a fusion of harmony and unpredictability, each element essential to the masterpiece we compose as we live. Every decision we make, like a note in a symphony, contributes to the larger composition, even if we don't always see the whole pattern immediately.

Just as music's movements ebb and flow, so too do our lives unfold with twists and turns that create something rich, nuanced, and beautiful. Music may be perceived as spontaneous as we listen to the melody, but it follows an ordered structure. Like a symphony's opening notes, birth is sometimes chaotic, unpredictable, and beyond our control, yet it holds a hidden order that gradually emerges.

As someone who appreciates both art and science, I believe music (as an artistic expression) and science (as an intellectual expression) come together in a way that invites us to appreciate and understand what life is about.

Incidentally, throughout this book, I use examples from artistic and scientific studies to help us better appreciate and understand the paradoxical aspects of our world. I also look for metaphors to help me explain things more fully.

In a symphony, instruments play off one another, sometimes in harmony and tension, creating a complex and dynamic whole. Similarly, life's early moments are shaped by forces that may seem random or chaotic yet ultimately contribute to who we become. No matter how small, every influence becomes part of the greater composition of who we are.

1 - Birth as a Symphony

In life, as in music, unpredictability does not mean a lack of structure. Instead, it points to a complexity that stretches beyond our immediate perception, an intricate dance between order and surprise where growth and discovery flourish. By exploring these chaotic beginnings, we question fate and free will.

Are we destined to become a certain way, or do we shape our lives through our choices? Fate offers comfort by suggesting a design behind life's randomness, yet true meaning arises from the actions we choose to take. Our lives, like music, are enriched by each crescendo, pause, and resolution.

Ancient Philosophies

Since ancient times, philosophers have wrestled with questions of fate, choice, and purpose. Epicurus, for example, saw the universe as a realm of chance, a place where events unfold without preordained purpose. In contrast, the Stoics believed that life had an underlying rational order, a structure that governs all events; they advocated for control over one's responses to life's circumstances rather than control over the circumstances themselves. Aristotle took a middle path, emphasizing human agency and viewing life's unpredictability as an invitation for personal growth.

These philosophies laid the groundwork for modern existentialist ideas. Modern existentialism revolves around themes of freedom, responsibility, authenticity, meaning, and the nature of existence in a world that may lack inherent purpose.

Jean-Paul Sartre asserted that "existence precedes essence." He suggested that we are born without a fixed purpose and define ourselves through actions. We're not bound by fate; we create meaning through our choices. In the symphony of birth, we see this idea illustrated. We enter the world as a blend of inherited qualities, environmental influences, and raw potential, and our lives become masterpieces we compose with each decision and experience.

Chaos & Order

Birth embodies this intricate complexity—a human dance of chaos and order, each playing a role in shaping our identity. From the moment we are born, we are thrust into a world of choices, challenges, and opportunities for growth. And much like a symphony, life does not stop after the first note; it continues to unfold, with each phase building upon the last. Our choices, like notes in a melody, are woven together to create a life that is uniquely our own.

While it's relatively easy to fear life's unpredictability, we can learn to embrace it—and not all at once. The true beauty of life lies in the balance between the known and the unknown, between what we can control and what we cannot. Life's challenges and surprises are not obstacles to our journeys but integral parts, helping us build strength, compassion, and understanding. Every crescendo of joy and every dissonance of hardship adds depth to our personal symphonies, enriching the experience of living our lives.

Conscious Engagement

Much like a musician engaged with their instrument, finding fulfillment in life comes from actively engaging with its rhythms, not from seeking complete control. We find fulfillment not by resisting change or seeking to control every outcome but by being open to the journey.

The magic of life lies in its unpredictability and ability to surprise, challenge, and inspire us. When we allow ourselves to be swept up by life's symphony, we hear its deeper harmonies, the subtle rhythms that guide us forward and reveal our true potential.

Ralph Waldo Emerson said, "Life is a journey, not a destination." Just as a symphony is experienced moment by moment, life unfolds in a series of interconnected events, each a note contributing to the larger whole. This journey of living is an ongoing experience shaped by the harmonious interplay of chance, choice, and change.

The Great Adventure

As Helen Keller once said, "Life is either a daring adventure or nothing."

This sentiment serves as a fitting reminder that we are each on a unique journey, shaped by our choices, actions, and responses to the unknown. Like a symphony, life is an adventure best experienced

1 - Birth as a Symphony

with an open heart and a spirit willing to embrace both the highs and lows.

Viewing life as a symphony reminds us that each phase, challenge, and joy adds richness and texture to our existence. The unpredictability of life, far from something to fear, becomes something to celebrate. We find our strength, creativity, and resilience in the surprises and the unknowns. In this way, we see that life's true meaning is not found in arriving at a destination but in embracing the journey, each step filled with potential, purpose, and beauty.

The Symphony Continues

One thing is for certain: our lives will continue to present us with challenges, crescendos of joy, and moments of quiet reflection. No single note, choice, or moment defines us; rather, the sum of our experiences shapes who we become. Like a great symphony, our lives are shaped by every twist, turn, note, and silence.

We may not always understand the symphony we are creating, but we can trust in its unfolding, knowing that most experiences add to the richness of our journey. Just as musicians must practice, learn, and adapt, we should also fully engage with life, embracing the order and chaos that shape our paths. As we continue, we will find that our lives, like music, hold an infinite potential for growth, change, and fulfillment.

As Helen Keller said, this is our great adventure—the journey of our existence—and ours to embrace.

Embracing Life's Journey

Like fire refining metal, pain purifies, distilling the essence of who we are and revealing depths unseen. Through pain, we must try to learn empathy's tender touch, gratitude for joy, and the strength to rise again. Through the lens of suffering, we see life's contrasts, light and shadow, each moment teaching us that even in hurt, there is healing and profound beauty in struggle.

Chapter 2: Positive Pain & Building Resilience

"Out of suffering have emerged the strongest souls; the most massive characters are seared with scars."

— *Kahlil Gibran*

Gibran's words reflect the transformative power of suffering, revealing how pain and hardship shape us, often from our earliest moments. The experience of pain—particularly the trauma of birth—imprints on us a profound will to survive and thrive. Pain is not merely something to endure; sometimes, it offers us a path to strength, wisdom, and empathy.

From the beginning, pain is a necessary challenge, not just for the newborn but also for the mother. For many, the journey from womb to world is the first encounter with struggle, requiring adaptability. Pain becomes part of our lives, like resistance that strengthens muscles. Our emotional resilience grows when we meet life's difficult moments with courage and honesty. Resilience is a recurrent theme in my writing. The word comes from the Latin verb *resilire*, meaning "to leap back" or "to recoil." You'll also see a lot of such trivia in my work.

The German philosopher

Friedrich Nietzsche (right, 1844–1900) emphasized pain's importance when he famously stated, "That which does not kill us makes us stronger." Originally from Twilight of the Idols (1888), his message speaks to the enduring human capacity to overcome adversity. Though now widely echoed as a motivational saying, Nietzsche's insight points to resilience as a defining aspect of our character, a quality forged by enduring hardship.

Encountering difficulty, even at an early age, fosters our capacity to cope with life's inevitable challenges. Whether through illness, loss, or failure, these experiences act like weights that strengthen the "muscles." This hardship is not merely about survival; it shapes us, molding our character and stretching our limits in ways we may not fully appreciate until later in life.

Kahlil Gibran eloquently likens pain to a "breaking of the shell that encloses your understanding," suggesting that suffering deepens our awareness and broadens our perspective.

His imagery conjures a delicate shell around the mind, protecting a person from the full depth of life's complexities. This shell symbolizes our current level of understanding, our comfort zone, where we grasp only a limited view of the world. Cracks form in this shell when we experience pain or suffering, exposing us to what lies beyond our familiar boundaries.

Through these cracks, we begin to see more of life's realities, some of which may be uncomfortable or

2 - Positive Pain & Building Resilience

challenging. Pain, while difficult, serves as a force that breaks open this shell, pushing us beyond our previous limits. In this way, suffering doesn't just cause harm but also expands and deepens our awareness. As the shell breaks, we gain new insights, becoming more empathetic and compassionate toward ourselves and others.

With each painful experience, the shell further dissolves, revealing a broader and wiser perspective. This painful process ultimately opens us to the richness of understanding on the other side, showing us that suffering can reveal truths we might never encounter.

Pain, like heat applied to metal, forges us, not by hardening us but by strengthening our capacity to endure and adapt. We find ourselves better prepared for life's challenges, which gives us the courage to meet adversity.

I once collaborated with an 88-year-old choreographer, Frank Regan, on a music video I produced. We took a break from the video shoot and started talking about dieting. I expressed frustration in my challenge to diet because I was always hungry. Frank told me more than a decade ago: "You have to learn not just to tolerate your hunger pains but to embrace them."

Beyond resilience, pain has the unique ability to foster empathy. Experiencing suffering—whether through heartbreak, physical illness, or disappointment—sensitizes us to the struggles of others, connecting us in our shared vulnerability. This understanding builds compassion, transforming our pain into a bridge to others. Empathy allows us to connect more deeply with others, making pain bearable and meaningful, as it creates bonds that foster community and support.

If you can see your pain as part of a shared human experience, it can strengthen your sense of belonging. Often, through our scars, we recognize one another, drawing closer because we realize, at a personal level, the tenacity that is sometimes required to face life's challenges. By connecting with others in this way, we transform suffering into an opportunity for kindness and solidarity, strengthening the fabric of our communities.

With suffering comes wisdom. Pain can force us to let go of unrealistic expectations, encouraging us to accept life as it is rather than as we wish it to be. This acceptance is not resignation but a grounded recognition that life includes suffering.

The Stoics believed in this principle, using the practice of prohairesis (moral choice) to guide responses to pain. Rather than seeking to avoid pain altogether, they embraced it as an opportunity to cultivate strength.

The well-known Serenity Prayer embodies this philosophy, asking for "the serenity to accept the things I cannot change, courage to change the things I can, and wisdom to know the difference." This prayer captures the essence of acceptance, encouraging us to meet life's complexities with humility and grace.

By understanding what is within our control, we can face pain without additional suffering brought on by resistance or denial. Acceptance, in this way, becomes a powerful tool for navigating life's challenges.

Heraclitus (c. 500 BCE), the ancient Greek philosopher, famously observed that opposites are essential for understanding reality. Similarly, the Taoist yin-yang philosophy teaches us that light and dark, pleasure and pain, are complementary forces that create harmony in life.

When we experience suffering, we're pushed beyond our comfort zones. This often leads to unexpected growth. Major challenges, such as the end of a relationship, the loss of a loved one, or failure in an endeavor, force us to confront our limitations and weaknesses. Overcoming these difficulties fosters self-awareness, transforming struggles into catalysts for growth.

Physical pain may become more common as we age, adding to life's inevitable discomforts. But even as our bodies change, we learn to adapt. Those who can make peace with their limitations often find pleasure despite discomfort. In this way, pain teaches us resilience and the value of acceptance and adaptability. It encourages us to adjust our mindset, focusing less on the discomfort and more on the richness of the life we continue to experience.

Accepting pain does not mean we welcome suffering. Rather, it helps us adapt based on limitations and acknowledge suffering as a natural part of life. Pain becomes less daunting when we see it as temporary and integral to our journey. Acceptance is a pathway to peace, helping us understand that a meaningful life isn't free of pain and that we strive to grow despite it. Pain opens us to self-discovery; through this discovery, we find strength we may not have known we had.

Just as Gibran suggests, pain breaks our understanding, allowing us to evolve in ways that joy alone cannot. Pain strips away superficial desires and comforts, revealing what truly matters. It compels us to examine our beliefs, fears, and values inwardly. Through this process, we uncover reserves of inner strength, discovering that we can face insurmountable challenges.

Pain often teaches us what comfort cannot: It pushes us to rise above our circumstances, helping us to see life's richness even amid hardship. In this way, pain strengthens us and transforms us, revealing layers of our character that remain hidden until tested.

And Then There's Fear

As a teenager, I was chopping wood, and the axe slipped, hitting my foot. At first, I felt no pain at all.

Embracing Life's Journey

For a moment, I hoped I might have been lucky, that perhaps my shoe had absorbed the impact. But when I took off the shoe and saw blood, everything changed. Suddenly, I was fully aware of the injury, and that's when the pain hit me. It was as if my fear had flipped a switch, amplifying the sensation.

Fear can be useful—it alerts us to danger—but it can also distort our perception, making a situation seem more dire than it is. Managing that fear is crucial so it doesn't intensify the pain or cloud our judgment when we need clarity.

Ironically, pain can also lead to a deeper sense of gratitude. When we emerge from hardship, we often appreciate life's simpler pleasures—a quiet morning, the warmth of companionship, or the beauty of nature. By teaching us about life's fragility and unpredictability, we become more aware of those moments of peace and joy. This gratitude enriches our lives, helping us to live more fully and with greater awareness of what truly matters.

Just as a symphony is composed of high and low notes, so is life shaped by joy and sorrow, success and failure. The music of life gains its depth and richness from these contrasts, creating a composition as complex as beautiful.

By accepting pain as a necessary part of our journey, we can find peace in the realization that life's symphony includes all notes—the harmonious and the discordant. Each phase of life, each challenge, adds to our unique composition, shaping who we are and who we will become.

Embracing Life's Journey

Albert Einstein's vision of relativity shifts our gaze, revealing that moments bend, distances warp, and what we perceive as steady is fluid, ever-shifting. We are travelers in this vast expanse, bound by the pull of gravity yet liberated by the vastness of possibility. Each moment stretches and shrinks, influenced by our place, motion, and choices—showing us that reality is a dance of perspectives. In this cosmic web, we are both small and infinite, anchored and free, feeling the timeless pulse of the universe as it moves through us.

Chapter 3: The Relativity of Life - Einstein's Insights

Albert Einstein's theory of relativity reshaped physics and offered us a profound way to reflect on our experiences. He revealed that time and space are fluid—stretching and contracting in response to forces around them. This insight gives us a unique perspective on how our emotions, connections, and growth are similarly flexible, shifting as our perspectives and contexts change.

Consider how joyful moments feel fleeting while times of sorrow seem endless. Waiting for a diagnosis or an apology can feel excruciatingly slow while watching a sunset or hearing a child's laughter seem over in a blink. This relativity in our daily lives invites us to reconsider how we relate to time and our varied experiences, encouraging us to be present, even in moments we wish would pass quickly.

Our human experience of time varies based on emotions and circumstances. Waiting for important news feels like an eternity, while an evening with close friends vanishes in a heartbeat. Einstein's concept of time as subjective resonates in these instances, illustrating how our internal clocks are deeply tied to our mental states.

Similarly, emotional proximity does not always mirror physical distance. A dear friend living thousands of miles away may feel closer than someone we see daily but with whom we've grown emotionally distant. This relativity in relationships underscores the importance of presence, understanding, and the investment of time in fostering meaningful connections. Like Einstein's equations, relationships require balance and mutual exchange to remain in harmony.

Blink of an Eye

While Einstein's concept of relativity helps us perceive life's fleeting and transformative nature, an infant's awareness grows with time. Imagine a newborn suddenly grasping the strange and overwhelming concept of time. Its tiny body, barely accustomed to the rhythm of breath, senses the vastness of existence yet recognizes how fleeting its own time will be—a hundred years. The number sounds colossal, incomprehensible to the newborn—an eternity to be explored. But then the realization settles: in the grand symphony of the universe, a hundred years is no more than a single, fleeting note—a blink of an eye.

This revelation might bring a sense of urgency, a deep desire to cling to each passing moment. Though incapable of walking or speaking, the infant needs to cherish the warmth of its mother's arms, the gentle rhythm of her heartbeat, and the way light dances on the walls. Every moment becomes precious, not because it is long but impossibly short.

3 - The Relativity of Life - Einstein's Insights

The Fragility

Understanding the brevity of life at birth would be to understand its fragility. Each clock tick becomes a tiny loss, a step forward into an unknown future. Days will blur into nights, seasons will shift, and years will melt into decades—all rushing toward the inevitable conclusion. The infant would see time not as a limitless horizon but as a narrowing funnel, each second slipping away faster than the last. And yet this brevity gives life its meaning. The infant might ask, "If my time is but a blink of an eye, how do I fill it?"

Eternity Within Moments

Paradoxically, understanding time's brevity could awaken a profound appreciation for its depth. Even the smallest moments could expand into an infinite period. The first laugh, the first taste of sweetness, the first time feeling the sun on your skin—all of these become entire worlds to explore. Time may be finite, but the richness of experience stretches each moment into something timeless.

In its newfound wisdom, the infant might come to understand that time is not measured by its length but by its quality. A minute of wonder, love, or joy holds more than an hour of indifference. And so, the blink of an eye becomes not a tragedy but a gift—a concentrated burst of potential, a lifetime to be lived fully.

Time as a Shared Experience

The infant may also realize that time is not experienced alone. It flows like a river, connecting everyone it touches. While the infant's hundred years may feel like a blink, it overlaps with countless other lives, creating a tapestry of shared moments. A single life may be brief, but its ripples extend far beyond its span, touching others in ways that echo across time.

In this way, the infant's awareness of time's fleeting nature could foster a deep connection to others. If each life is a blink, then every shared smile, every act of kindness, becomes a way to make those blinks matter—a way to transcend the limits of an individual lifespan and become part of something enduring.

The Blink as a Miracle

Finally, the infant might marvel at the miracle of existing at all. In the infinity of time, to be alive, feel, think, love, even for a moment, is extraordinary. The blink of an eye is brief, but it contains everything. It is the music of the heart, the laughter of friends, the wisdom of old age, and the quiet peace of a life well-lived. To live for a hundred years may seem like nothing, but to live even one day fully is to have tasted eternity.

And so, the infant, cradled in its mother's arms, might close its eyes—not fearing time's passage, but in gratitude for the blink it has been given.

Einstein's concept of an expanding universe can serve as a metaphor for personal growth. As the cosmos stretches outward, creating space for new stars and galaxies, our lives expand with every

3 - The Relativity of Life - Einstein's Insights

experience, thought, and relationship. Each challenge we face adds layers to our character, like cosmic dust gathering to form new planets. This interconnectedness reminds us that we are not isolated entities but part of a grand, ever-evolving system.

Growth is not linear. Our inner emotional boundaries continuously stretch and contract, much like the universe itself. Personal growth often involves setbacks, plateaus, and unexpected leaps forward. These oscillations mirror the natural rhythms of stretching beyond our comfort zones and retreating inward to reflect and recharge.

Stretching involves pushing ourselves into unfamiliar territory—learning a new skill, facing fear, or embracing vulnerability. These moments challenge our resilience and expand our emotional capacity.

On the other hand, contracting periods allow us to process these changes, consolidate what we've learned, and prepare for the next stretch. This cyclical nature of growth respects our limits while fostering deeper, more meaningful progress.

Einstein believed the universe operated with an ordered logic, yet he struggled with the idea of determinism—that natural laws preordain everything. His famous quote, "God does not play dice with the universe," reflects his discomfort with randomness and the idea of a chaotic cosmos. Yet, he also acknowledged the human experience of free will and our ability to shape our paths.

This tension between fate and freedom resonates deeply. Are we mere players in a prewritten script, or do we hold the pen to write our own stories? Einstein's willingness to grapple with this paradox invites us to embrace uncertainty. By letting go of the need for absolute control, we can find peace in navigating life's mysteries.

Einstein's imaginative "thought experiments" were central to his groundbreaking discoveries. He transcended conventional limitations by visualizing scenarios rather than relying solely on mathematical equations. This approach underscores the power of creativity and visualization in problem-solving and personal growth.

Einstein famously said, "Imagination is more important than knowledge. For knowledge is limited, while imagination embraces the entire world." This belief encourages us to see obstacles as opportunities to envision new possibilities. Whether imagining a better future or reinterpreting past struggles, our creative minds can help us rewrite the narratives we live by.

Imagination enables us to transcend our immediate circumstances. It allows us to dream, innovate, and see beyond the constraints of our current reality. By nurturing this faculty, we open ourselves to a world of infinite possibilities and deepen our capacity for empathy, creativity, and resilience.

Einstein's insights into relativity are not just about physics; they offer profound lessons for life. As time and space are flexible, so is our capacity to adapt, grow, and find meaning in life's challenges. Resilience is, in many ways, a practice of emotional relativity—learning to bend without breaking, to stretch without snapping.

By embracing the fluidity of time, relationships, and growth, we can navigate life's uncertainties with greater grace. We learn that no moment, whether joyful or painful, lasts forever. This understanding

3 - The Relativity of Life - Einstein's Insights

empowers us to cherish the present and trust in the cyclical nature of life's ebb and flow.

Einstein's theory of relativity reshaped our knowledge of the universe, but its implications extend far beyond science. It teaches us that life, like the cosmos, is constantly changing by our perspectives and choices. Just as gravity bends light and time stretches near black holes, our experiences bend and stretch according to the forces we encounter.

Life is not static. It is a dynamic interplay of forces, a dance between chaos and order, freedom and fate, imagination and logic. By embracing this relativity, we find the courage to grow, the humility to accept life's mysteries, and the wisdom to navigate our ever-expanding journeys.

Time and space are twin mysteries, threads that weave the fabric of existence, holding us yet always just beyond our grasp. Together, they create the paradox of here and now keeping us in place yet urging us forward as we search for meaning in their endless dance, feeling their quiet tug toward a horizon we cannot see but endlessly pursue.

Chapter 4: Time & Space Conundrum

Einstein's theory of relativity, commonly represented by $E=mc^2$, fundamentally transformed our understanding of the universe. This equation demonstrates the relationship between energy (E), mass (m), and the speed of light (c).

In essence, $E=mc^2$ reveals that energy and mass are interchangeable, meaning that under certain conditions, energy can transform into mass and vice versa. This concept, which seems like a cosmic magic trick, explains why stars can burn for billions of years and how nuclear energy is released.

Instead of considering space and time as separate entities, Einstein combined them into a single four-dimensional fabric called space-time. In this model, gravity is not a force but a result of Space-Time curving around massive objects.

To better understand this concept, let's take a brief journey through four geometric dimensions:

1. **First Dimension**: A simple line that can be measured in length. Any position on this line can be described using a single number indicating its distance from a starting point (the origin).

2. **Second Dimension**: A plane with length and width, such as a drawing on paper. Every point on this plane can be located using x and y coordinates.

3. **Third Dimension**: A space with length, width, and height, giving objects volume. It is represented geometrically with three coordinates: x, y, and z.

4. **Fourth Dimension**: Space-Time, which incorporates length, width, height, and time. Unlike the first three dimensions, time adds a dynamic element, representing each moment as a "slice" of 3D space.

Here's an analogy: Imagine a film strip where each frame is a 3D scene snapshot. Each frame represents a moment in time, and together, they form a 4D structure. Similarly, Space-Time is like a stack of 3D "slices" representing every position and moment in the universe. Although we cannot fully visualize 4D shapes with our 3D minds, mathematicians use projections to represent them. In this framework, objects are no longer static but part of a continuous journey through space and time, shaping our understanding of motion, gravity, and other fundamental concepts in physics.

4 - Time & Space Conundrum

    To picture relativity, imagine Space-Time as a vast trampoline. Place a heavy object, like a bowling ball, on it, and the surface dips. A marble rolled nearby will curve toward the ball, like planets moving around a star. This visualization captures gravity in Einstein's universe—not as an invisible pull but as a natural curve that objects follow.

    Everything—even time—is dynamic, responding to the mass and movement of objects. Together, time and space create the paradox of here and now, holding us in place while urging us forward, pulling us toward a horizon we cannot see but are endlessly drawn to pursue.

    Einstein's theory of relativity challenges the simplicity of time as a linear flow and space as a constant framework. Instead, they are interwoven, flexible, and responsive to our experiences.

Aging with Time & Space

As we age, our relationship with time and space evolves. Places that once seemed vast now feel smaller, anchoring memories of who we were and who we've become. Revisiting old spaces can highlight our growth, showing how time transforms our connections to familiar environments.

Each phase of life—starting a new career, becoming a parent, or relocating—reshapes our mental and emotional landscapes. Memory blurs the boundaries of past, present, and future, giving us a non-linear experience of time. Revisiting familiar places or reconnecting with people from our past often transports us to another time, reminding us of life's cyclical nature.

4 - Time & Space Conundrum

Astronomer Carl Sagan (1934–1996) famously said, "We are made of star-stuff." This cosmic perspective encourages us to see ourselves as part of a vast cycle transcending individual lifetimes. Our bodies, formed from elements forged in stars, will one day return to the cosmos, reflecting the cyclical nature of existence.

Viewing life as part of a cosmic cycle helps us live in harmony with time and space, grounding us in the present moment where life unfolds.

Being Present

Understanding time and space as fluid invites us to cultivate mindfulness—the art of being present. When we appreciate the flexible nature of time, we focus less on rushing to the future or dwelling on the past. Instead, we engage fully with each experience, finding beauty in the here and now.

Moments that once seemed mundane can become meaningful, transforming our daily lives. Embracing the fluidity of time and space allows us to savor life's richness and find gratitude in its small, fleeting joys.

Giving Life Meaning

Einstein's philosophy teaches us that life isn't about mastering every detail but about staying open, curious, and compassionate. The questions we ask, the connections we form, and the mysteries we encounter are what truly give life its depth and meaning. In this view, perfection is not the goal; instead, it's the process of seeking, learning, and adapting that defines our journey.

By living with wonder, exploring life's profound depths, and cherishing its fleeting moments of joy, we can navigate complexities with grace. Life transforms into a journey of discovery, where fulfillment lies not in reaching specific goals but in the experiences and growth along the way. When we let go of rigid expectations, we find beauty in the unexpected, and life becomes a dance of curiosity and acceptance.

Understanding time and space as fluid and flexible forces reminds us that life holds endless possibilities. Like the ever-expanding universe, we are continually shaped by our experiences, relationships, and personal transformations. This perspective bridges the scientific with the spiritual, encouraging us to embrace life with curiosity, gratitude, and an openness to the unknown. It's a reminder that change is not a threat but an invitation to evolve and grow.

Through this lens, we find that life isn't about certainty or control but about the beauty of exploration and the courage to embrace its infinite potential. Just as the universe thrives in balance between order and chaos, so too do our lives unfold most fully when we learn to harmonize intention with spontaneity. By welcoming both the known and the mysterious, we allow ourselves to truly expand.

To live with this perspective is to celebrate the interplay of opposites: structure and freedom, logic and wonder, self and other. Einstein's insights encourage us not only to think deeply but also to feel deeply, to connect, and to marvel at the sheer vastness of existence. This blend of science and spirit offers a timeless message: that the greatest journey is not outward but inward, toward understanding, connection, and love.

4 - Time & Space Conundrum

"A human being is part of the whole, called the universe by us, a part limited in time and space. He experiences himself, his thoughts, and feelings as something separate from the rest—a kind of optical delusion of his consciousness."
— *Albert Einstein*

Embracing Life's Journey

Spiritual guidance is a subtle compass rooted in intuition, flowing from within and beyond, urging us toward truth, compassion, and the mysteries of existence. It moves without words as light in dark places and warmth in cold spaces and leads us, not by certainty but by trust, nudging us to listen deeply, see beyond what is visible, and feel the presence of something greater.

Chapter 5: Spiritual Faith & Inner Guidance

As I contemplated, wrote, and edited this book, I was conflicted about whether or to what extent I should focus on where spiritual beliefs come into play vis-à-vis the topics I'm discussing. You see, I don't subscribe to certain mainstream ideas about the Judeo-Christian God. I have my ideas, instead. Yet, I don't want readers to turn away because we have different views and beliefs about supreme beings. Regardless of my views, religion plays an important role in most cultures. So, I acknowledge the need to tread thoughtfully and carefully in this chapter.

While these pages touch on religious faith, the book does not rely on religious principles. While the general principles of spirituality often align with my ideas, the book's broader themes are not rooted solely in faith in a supreme being or spiritual entity. This work invites you to consider these ideas independently, with or without a belief in a higher power, and to engage with the reflections in a way that
resonates with your experiences.

Early Curiosity

I grew up in a family whose members didn't necessarily believe in God or practice organized religion. My parents never took us to church or participated in religious ceremonies. Nonetheless, I was always curious about what faith meant to other people, especially because friends at school talked about their church experiences. In high school, I often went to church with my friends to understand what they were experiencing. I didn't feel drawn to any belief, but I wanted to better understand what meant so much to them. Attending church gave me a window into different ways of thinking about life and purpose, even though church involvement wasn't a part of my family's routine.

Something changed one summer when we came up from Florida to visit my grandma in New Jersey. My mother, who had always been somewhat agnostic, suddenly announced to my dad that she wanted my brother and me to be baptized "just to make sure." To this day, I'm not entirely certain what prompted her change of heart. Perhaps it was her version of spirituality, a precaution against the unknown. I was around twelve, and my brother was five, so we didn't fully understand the gravity of my mother's decision. Still, I recall feeling a sense of excitement mixed with curiosity.

During one trip leaving New Jersey to return to Florida, my

5 - Spiritual Faith & Inner Guidance

mother decided it was time, so we turned into a random Lutheran church. The stop at this church was spontaneous, unplanned, and a bit surreal. However, the experience was defining, even though I don't know the church's location. We were baptized on the spot—a quick, unceremonious ritual that left me feeling like I'd been anointed by something significant, even if I couldn't define what that was.

Years later, after I'd married and had my daughter, I thought about the day we pulled into a church in New Jersey. I was living in northern New Jersey, and having my daughter made me want to reconnect with that part of my story. I decided to take a drive to see if I could find the church as if finding it would tie together these fragments of belief, memory, and family legacy. My daughter, wife, and I headed out to see if I could find the church.

Strangely, the car seemed to guide us directly to the church as if it knew the way. I was struck by familiarity when I arrived as if the church had been waiting for me to return. It was one of those moments that felt like a miracle, a serendipitous event that seemed too meaningful to ignore. Standing in front of that church with my daughter in my arms, I felt connected to something larger, a force that had gently woven this experience into my life.

We went inside, where my daughter and wife were baptized, bringing the journey that began in my childhood full circle. It wasn't about converting to a religion or committing to a particular faith. It was about honoring the feeling of a guiding presence in my life, something beyond my understanding that led me back to the church. It was one of many moments in my life that felt like small miracles, moments that, over time, became the basis of my spiritual belief.

Serendipity & Faith

As I grew older, I began taking notice of these small miracles, unexpected encounters that seemed to carry a deeper meaning. I started to believe that life guided us and that there were forces at work we couldn't see or fully comprehend. While I may not have adopted a traditional sense of God, my spirituality grew from these serendipitous experiences. They seemed to urge me toward certain places, people, and decisions. Although such moments weren't always dramatic, they stayed with me, shaping my view of the world and helping me embrace life's journey.

These experiences also taught me that spirituality doesn't have to fit into a specific doctrine or belief system. It can simply be a quiet awareness of the mysterious and the miraculous in everyday life. The feeling that something greater is at play, even if we can't name or understand it, became a comfort and inspiration for me. For some, such a feeling stems from their faith in God; for others, it is tied to a sense of universal connection, intuition, or inner wisdom. Whatever our spirituality connects us to, it invites us to trust our journeys and be open to the unexpected.

Unexpected Miracles

Looking back, I realize my mother's spontaneous decision to have us baptized wasn't about subscribing to a particular belief. It was her way of acknowledging the unknown and saying, "Just in case." Perhaps that's what faith is: a willingness to believe, just in case, and a gentle openness to the possibility of something greater.

Ultimately, each of us builds our beliefs based on our unique experiences. My path to spirituality has been a mosaic of small moments, often unplanned and sometimes bewildering. These small moments have shaped my sense of purpose and connection. I believe that these experiences, these "miracles" of my life, are not just chances but rather part of a guiding presence that helps me find meaning, especially when life becomes challenging or uncertain.

Every Day Miracles

I hope you find something meaningful, no matter what you believe. Faith, spirituality, and serendipity aren't about strict definitions or doctrines. They're about finding your compass, your way of making sense of the journey. Whether religious, spiritual, agnostic, or simply open to life's mysteries, you may find inspiration here to embrace your journey with curiosity, courage, and gratitude.

5 - Spiritual Faith & Inner Guidance 44

"In faith there is enough light for those who want to believe and enough shadows to blind those who don't."
— *Blaise Pascal*

Embracing Life's Journey

Life touches us through our senses, painting reality with colors, sounds, scents, and textures that awaken us to the world's depth and beauty. Each sensation is a doorway, an invitation to experience life fully, to feel the warmth of sunlight on the skin, to taste the sharp sweetness of ripe fruit, and to lose ourselves in music's embrace. The senses stir our emotions, connect us to memory, and bring awareness to the present moment.

Chapter 6: Stimulating Senses & Emotional Awareness

Our first encounter with life comes through sensation, often through the discomfort and shock of birth, explored in the first chapter. From birth, our senses connect us to the world, revealing its beauty and challenges. Sensory experiences—whether overwhelming or subtle—shape our emotional and intellectual growth, grounding us in the present and heightening our appreciation for life's richness. Sight reveals beauty, color, and form; sound brings music, language, and emotion; and touch connects us physically to our surroundings. Taste and smell evoke strong memories linked to people, places, and moments that matter. Embracing these sensory experiences deepens our connection to the world, enhancing our sense of presence and vitality. Yet, modern life often floods us with sensory input—digital notifications, endless screens, and constant noise—that dulls our sensitivity, making it harder to savor life's day-to-day wonders truly.

In our fast-paced, digitally connected world, overstimulation is one of the greatest challenges to our senses. With screens and digital distractions constantly vying for our attention, our senses are often bombarded, making it difficult to fully engage with any single experience. This constant barrage can cause us to overlook the small, precious details around us—the warmth of sunlight on our skin, the subtle fragrance of a flower, or the feeling of fresh air filling our lungs. Our senses can be buried beneath the noise, distancing us from ourselves, others, and the present moment. During these experiences, we can also begin to tune out the noise. The risk is that tuning out the noise may lead us to tune out everything to the point that we become comfortably numb.

Practicing mindfulness is an alternative to tuning out noise to the point of numbness. Focusing on everyday experiences like savoring a meal, listening to music without distraction, or talking with a friend helps us reconnect with the present moment. These mindful practices remind us of the beauty in life's simplicity, encouraging us to tune back into our surroundings. By consciously shifting our attention from the digital world to the physical one, we notice the colors, sounds, and textures that often get overlooked. I fall into the trap of multitasking more than I'd like—eating dinner while watching

6 - Stimulating Senses & Emotional Awareness 48

a show or answering emails while conversing. In a world of constant distractions, reconnecting with our senses by paying attention to the "here and now" moments helps ground us in what truly matters.

While our five physical senses help us navigate the world, intangible senses—intuition, emotional perception, and spiritual awareness—shape our experience of life just as profoundly. These subtle senses connect us more deeply to ourselves and others, enhance our understanding, and enrich our interactions.

Often called a "sixth sense," intuition is the gut feeling that guides us when logic alone doesn't provide answers. The sense tells us which path to take or who to trust, even when we don't have all the facts. When we listen to our intuition, we tap into the inner wisdom that often knows what's best for us, even before our conscious minds do.

If we are open to active listening, emotional perception may enable us to pick up on the feelings of others, building empathy and deepening our connections. This sense allows us to read between words and actions and hear the emotions beneath the surface. Emotional perception can help us relate more genuinely, enabling us to offer support, compassion, and understanding to those around us.

Spiritual awareness provides a sense of connection to something greater than ourselves, whether it's a divine presence, the universe, or a deep inner peace. This sense transcends the physical and allows us to find meaning and purpose in life, profoundly helping us feel grounded and connected to the world. Spiritual awareness reminds us of our place in the broader tapestry of existence and allows us to cultivate gratitude and a sense of belonging. These intangible senses guide our decision-making and add depth to our lives. Yet, in a world of

6 - Stimulating Senses & Emotional Awareness

distractions, losing touch with them is easy. By nurturing these senses through practices like meditation, journaling, or simply spending quiet time in nature, we enhance our connection to ourselves and others, allowing these inner senses to thrive.

Helen Keller, who was both blind and deaf, captured the essence of sensory experience better than most. She said, "The best and most beautiful things in the world cannot be seen or even touched—they must be felt with the heart." Keller's wisdom teaches us that the most meaningful sensory experiences often go beyond the physical. They reside in the intangible spaces of love, connection, and presence, enriching our lives in ways that sight or sound alone cannot.

While this chapter emphasizes the importance of embracing natural sensory experiences, it's also important to acknowledge the risks of artificial stimulants like drugs and alcohol, which can distort our perceptions. These substances offer temporary escapes or highs, but often at the cost of dulling our natural senses over time. Eventually, rather than seeking artificial means to heighten my senses, I tried safer methods to expand my sensory awareness. Meditation, therapy, creative expression, and physical exercise helped me tap into the beauty of life without the downsides of artificial stimulants. These practices cultivate mindfulness and connection to the world around me.

Mindfulness is focusing one's attention on the present moment with an attitude of openness, curiosity, and acceptance. I practice mindfulness by taking "Life Pauses"—short breaks from what I'm doing to spend time outdoors in the garden, listen to jazz, or call my daughter. Finding your mindful pauses can create a foundation for peace and joy. This sensory symphony is available to us at any moment, waiting for us to pause, notice, and listen. We should remember that life's greatest treasures often lie not in what we achieve but in what we experience. Helen Keller's words ring true: "The best and most beautiful things in the world cannot be seen or even touched—they must be felt with the heart."

6 - Stimulating Senses & Emotional Awareness

"When the power of love overcomes the love of power the world will know peace."

– *Jimi Hendrix*

Embracing Life's Journey

To judge, evaluate, and measure—these are the mind's attempts to make sense of life's vast complexity, to shape the intangible and sometimes tangible into something known. Yet, in the precision of each judgment, in the calculated measure, lies both clarity and limitation, for some truths slip past reason's grasp, too deep, too mysterious to be confined by our scales and standards. As we weigh the world around us, we must ask ourselves: do we diminish what we measure?

Chapter 7: Judging, Evaluating & Letting Go

When I used to visit a counselor for my emotional issues, I learned that one aspect of my condition had a name: passive-aggressive behavior. It sounds impressive and much like one of the paradoxical aspects of life we keep talking about. Passive and aggressive—at the same time? I learned that instead of openly confronting someone, I would express anger or frustration through subtle actions, sarcasm, or veiled comments

According to my "shrink" of yesteryear, passive-aggressive behavior allowed me to express discontent or revenge without engaging in a direct conflict, often because I wanted to avoid an argument or was uncomfortable with open confrontation. While this may seem like an example of anger, it's about being judgmental and exploring the possible consequences. I don't enjoy being measured, judged, or evaluated by anyone unless you have something positive about me. And yet, I do love expressing my critical perceptions of others, and I think I'm right most of the time. What's wrong with me?

So much of our energy goes into measuring, judging, and evaluating, but does it help us? Habits like these can be draining, leaving us distracted, tired, and inadequate. Unfortunately, our lives today are fixated on comparison—appearance, achievement, and status.

What if we could let go of this constant evaluation and focus instead on living more authentically? While judgment is deeply rooted in human nature, we can find a pathway to freedom by balancing discernment with acceptance.

Indeed, judgment and comparison have long been essential for our survival. Our ancestors needed to assess their environment for danger, evaluate trustworthiness, and make quick judgments that often meant life or death. Physical dangers have largely diminished today, but this instinct to compare has shifted toward evaluating success, social status, and personal worth. Rather than feeling more connected, constant comparison often leaves us feeling inadequate or superior—both emotionally draining states that disconnect us from others and ourselves.

7 - Judging, Evaluating & Letting Go 56

Let's get some advice from the professionals about this subject. In 1954, psychologist Leon Festinger introduced the Social Comparison Theory, which suggests that we gauge our worth and status by comparing ourselves to others. Festinger explained that when we look up to those more successful or accomplished, we might feel inadequate; when we look down on others, we might feel a temporary boost of self-worth, but it can also foster a sense of false superiority.

While comparison can sometimes inspire us to strive for growth, it often becomes a cycle that keeps us fixated on external validation and hinders our self-acceptance. Today, we know that judging others often gives us a feeling of control in an unpredictable world. By categorizing people, situations, and experiences, we feel we've created structure and gained understanding. For example, comparing our finances to a friend's might bring brief reassurance, but soon, we find ourselves caught up in a new comparison. These judgments are often fleeting and ultimately add little real value, sometimes leaving us with more anxiety and uncertainty.

Our judgments and evaluations often stem from the ego's need to feel secure and validated. When we feel insecure, comparing ourselves to others offers temporary relief but may leave us even more anxious. We constantly judge others and evaluate ourselves, but why?

Did I do enough today? Am I good enough? This self-judgment exhausts and drains energy that could be used more meaningfully, like nurturing relationships or pursuing passions.

One of the most exhausting forms of judgment is perfectionism because it demands that we meet impossible standards and leave no room for mistakes or growth. Perfectionism is driven by a fear of being judged and failing; it is often fueled by the idea that our worth is tied

7 - Judging, Evaluating & Letting Go

to flawless performances. The pursuit of perfection is endless, leading to burnout, disappointment, and a persistent feeling of inadequacy.

Meanwhile, social media has intensified our natural tendency to compare. Platforms like Instagram, Facebook, and Twitter allow us to see the carefully curated highlights of others' lives, making it nearly impossible not to feel inadequate. I know this firsthand—I manage around seventy-five Facebook groups, and scrolling through people's highlights every day can be overwhelming.

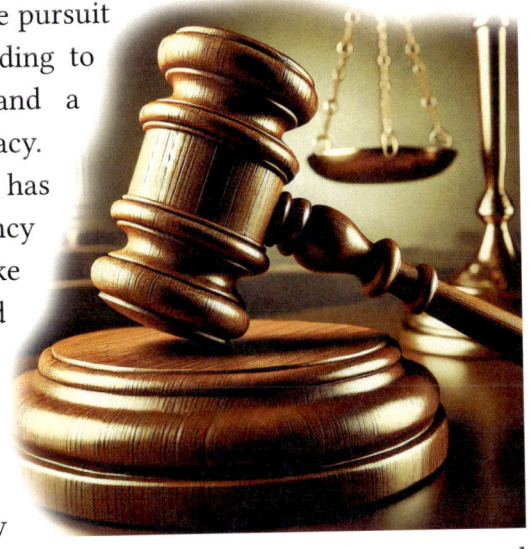

These curated glimpses into others' lives show only the best moments, often leaving us with a skewed perspective that traps us in a loop of comparison. The reality is that everyone has struggles, setbacks, and imperfections that remain hidden behind their social media feed. We should avoid constantly measuring ourselves against others, even subconsciously, because we can create a sense of disconnection, pushing us further from a life rooted in authenticity.

How do we break free from the cycle of judgment and comparison? By consciously shifting our attention to the present moment, we shift our focus from overthinking and comparing to engaging fully with what is happening now. By appreciating what we have, we create a sense of fulfillment rooted in contentment, freeing ourselves from the need to measure up.

Treat yourself with the same kindness and understanding you would offer a friend. Remember that no one is perfect, and you don't have to be either. By showing compassion to ourselves, we become less reliant on others' approval and find validation from within. By focusing on your unique path, reviewing where you have been and where you are headed, and correcting your course when necessary, you can find fulfillment in your personal growth.

The ancient philosophy of Yin and Yang embodies a balance between judgment and acceptance. Judgment is not inherently negative; it serves a purpose when balanced with compassion and understanding. Yin represents qualities like acceptance, reflection, and allowing things to be, while Yang embodies action, ambition, and evaluation. Knowing when to judge and when to let go conserves our energy and makes living with greater harmony and balance more possible. Believe me, letting go of judgment is liberating!

When we free ourselves from judgment, we can embrace life as it is, appreciating our experiences without attaching labels or expectations. This acceptance helps us focus less on perfection and more on presence, finding joy in simply living. It does not mean eliminating discernment or personal standards. Rather, it's about finding a balance that enables us to live with kindness toward ourselves and others.

We create a rich, meaningful, and deeply connected life by cultivating gratitude, acceptance, and authentic living. Letting go of judgment allows us to live with grace, compassion, and inner harmony, finding peace in the present moment and joy in the simple act of living.

7 - Judging, Evaluating & Letting Go

"As I approach the end of my life, I have even less and less interest in examining what have got to be very superficial evaluations or opinions about the significance of one's life or one's work. I was never given to it when I was healthy, and I am less given to it now."

– Leonard Cohen

Intuition whispers what reason cannot explain—a feeling, a flash of insight, a path sensed rather than seen. Intuitive rationalization is the dance between the known and the mysterious, where instinct leads and logic then follows. It is the art of justifying what we feel deeply, finding words for what the soul already understands, and building bridges between impulse and thought. In these moments, we realize that some truths need no proof and that sometimes we trust without reason.

Chapter 8: Harnessing Intuitive Rationalization

Psychologist Carl Jung (depicted with a floating pipe) dove deeply into the subconscious and once remarked, "Intuition does not denote something contrary to reason, but something outside the province of reason." This insight captures the essence of intuitive rationalization, a term I coined years ago to describe the dynamic interaction between intuition and rational thought. It suggests that intuition operates beyond the boundaries of pure logic, guiding us through a subconscious process that often eludes rational explanation. While we might later rationalize our decisions, the initial impulse often comes from a place that reason alone can't fully reach.

Understanding this interplay between intuition and rationalization helps us appreciate how our instincts shape our actions, even as we search for logical explanations to validate them. Intuition and rationalization represent two distinct yet interconnected processes that shape how we make decisions and justify our actions.

Intuition is the "gut feeling"—a quick, automatic response influenced by past experiences, emotions, and subconscious associations. It's an instinctual process that often kicks in, creating a sense of knowing that we may not be able to explain fully. For example, meeting someone for the first time and immediately trusting them, even without clear evidence, is an act of intuition.

Rationalization, on the other hand, happens afterward. It's the logical explanation we create to justify a decision we've already made. Often, we generate reasons for why we acted as we did, even when our initial choice was driven by intuition or emotion. For instance, after buying something expensive on impulse, you might rationalize by saying, "I deserved to treat myself," even though the decision stemmed from an emotional response. In short, intuition often comes first—a quick, instinctive reaction. Rationalization follows, helping us make sense of our actions by providing them with a logical framework.

I first discovered—or perhaps invented—the concept of intuitive rationalization while developing my magical card tricks. Magic is a fascinating example of how intuition and rationalization work together for the magician and the audience.

8 - Harnessing Intuitive Rationalization

As a magician, you rely on intuition to read your audience, sensing when to misdirect or when to reveal a trick. This process is almost instinctual, developed through countless hours of practice and performance, where you build a gut-level understanding of human reactions. Magicians don't always analyze why a particular technique works; they know it does. Intuition in magic is about timing and audience awareness. A skilled magician senses the perfect moment to create suspense or execute a sleight of hand, even if they can't fully articulate why. The audience's attention, reactions, and subtle cues guide the performance, allowing the magician to intuitively "feel" the flow of the trick.

Embracing Life's Journey

After the trick is completed, rationalization often comes into play. The magician might attribute their success to specific techniques or skills, describing it as sleight of hand or expert timing. But in the heat of the performance, intuition guides the show, making each move feel natural and in sync with the audience. For the audience, intuitive rationalization works in reverse. They witness the magic and experience a sense of wonder, even if the trick defies logic. Their intuition tells them something extraordinary has happened, but their minds quickly seek explanations. They might think, "Maybe he had something hidden in his sleeve," or "It was probably mirrors," as they try to rationalize the impossible.

Carl Jung argued that intuition is not the opposite of reason but a complementary process that can reveal deeper truths. Intuition allows us to access insights that logic alone cannot always reach, often

8 - Harnessing Intuitive Rationalization

guiding us toward decisions that feel "right" even if we can't fully articulate why. In moments of crisis or urgency, intuition helps us make quick decisions based on accumulated knowledge and subconscious awareness. Later, rationalization fills in the gaps, offering a logical framework that makes our decisions seem more coherent.

Consider someone who changes careers because "it just felt right." They may not have a detailed plan or fully rationalized explanation, but they feel a strong internal pull. Later, they may rationalize this choice by listing logical benefits—such as better pay or new growth opportunities—yet the true motivation was rooted in intuition. In this case, rationalization helps reinforce the decision, providing a structure for what was initially a gut-driven choice.

Over-Rationalization

While rationalization can provide structure and reassurance, it can also lead to self-deception. When we over-rationalize, we may ignore our intuition in favor of logical explanations that don't align with our true feelings. This tendency to over-rationalize often arises when we feel uncomfortable or uncertain. We avoid confronting deeper emotional truths by creating logical reasons for our actions.

In relationships, for instance, over-rationalization can lead us to ignore red flags or warning signs. A person might intuitively sense that their partner isn't trustworthy yet rationalize their behavior by saying, "Everyone makes mistakes," or "They're going through a tough time." This rationalization may temporarily ease the discomfort but ultimately prevents us from making decisions that honor our well-being.

To avoid the pitfalls of over-rationalization, it's essential to cultivate self-awareness. By regularly checking in with our intuitive responses, we can recognize when our rationalizations might be masking deeper issues. Honoring our intuition doesn't mean dismissing logic; it means using rational thought to support, rather than override, our gut instincts.

8 - Harnessing Intuitive Rationalization

Finding Balance

There are times when rationalization becomes essential, particularly in complex situations that require careful thought and analysis. It's important to evaluate the pros and cons, consider different perspectives, and weigh potential outcomes. All these things help us make well-informed choices. When we approach decisions with clarity and intention, we can better enhance our ability to make choices that align with our goals and values.

Intuitive rationalization is not about choosing one process over the other but recognizing when each is appropriate. By developing a nuanced understanding of intuition and rationalization, we can better navigate life, knowing when to trust our instincts and when to apply deliberate thought.

Cultivating Intuition

One of the most effective ways to develop intuitive rationalization is to cultivate a stronger connection with your intuition. Intuition often speaks through subtle cues—feelings, images, or sensations that arise without conscious thought. We can better understand our inner guidance by paying attention to these cues. Meditation, journaling, and mindfulness can help us tune into our intuition.

Meditation quiets the mind, allowing us to hear our inner voice without the interference of rational thought. Writing in a journal allows us to explore our thoughts and feelings, helping us identify patterns that reveal our intuitive insights. Mindfulness brings our awareness to the present moment, allowing us to notice our intuition's subtle signals.

Ultimately, intuitive rationalization is not about achieving perfection but about cultivating awareness. It's a journey of self-discovery, where we learn to trust ourselves and make choices that resonate with our true selves. By integrating intuition and rationalization, we open ourselves to a life of authenticity, depth, and meaning, guided by the wisdom of both heart and mind.

8 - Harnessing Intuitive Rationalization

"The intuitive mind is a sacred gift and the rational mind is a faithful servant."

– Albert Einstein

Embracing Life's Journey

Forgiveness is a gentle release, an unburdening of the heart that ripples out like echoes in still water, softening the sharp edges of past hurts. It whispers of freedom for those forgiven and the forgiver, freeing space within where peace may grow. In the act of letting go, we invite healing to dance through old wounds, to quiet the ghosts of memory.

Chapter 9: Echoes of Forgiveness

Forgiveness is a word we hear often but rarely explore in depth. For some, it feels like a lofty ideal or moral duty; for others, it brings back memories of pain and betrayal. Yet true forgiveness is a deeply personal journey. It doesn't just let go of the past; it transforms the person who forgives. When we forgive—whether others or ourselves—we release the burdens that bind us to old wounds, creating space for growth, peace, and a more open future.

Forgiveness can feel like setting down a heavy bag we've carried for too long, filled with regrets, grudges, and grievances that have weighed us down. Often, we don't realize the toll until we finally let go. By releasing this weight, we open ourselves to the present and future, free from the shadows of past hurts.

Holding onto Anger

In my life, I've held onto anger toward people who mistreated, betrayed, or cheated me. At first, I would hold a grudge, but eventually, I'd find the anger fading, sometimes forgetting why I was angry. Holding onto resentment or regret can feel protective, as remembering past wrongs can shield us from being hurt again.

But over time, this protective shell hardens into a burden, limiting our capacity for compassion, joy, and meaningful connection.

Forgiveness frees us and others from the endless cycle of blame and judgment, liberating us from the past. It doesn't deny what happened; rather, it allows us to reclaim our peace, releasing control over someone else's actions and shifting focus back to our well-being.

Forgiveness isn't just an emotional or spiritual practice; science shows it profoundly affects the brain and body. Studies reveal that people who practice forgiveness tend to have lower levels of stress hormones like cortisol, improved immune function, and better cardiovascular health.

Resentment, on the other hand, has been linked to chronic stress, which can harm the heart, weaken immunity, and even accelerate aging. Neurological research indicates that when we forgive, our brains activate areas associated with empathy, compassion, and emotional regulation. Forgiveness rewires the brain, enabling us to respond to pain with understanding rather than retaliation. This shift doesn't just heal relationships; it heals us.

9 - Echoes of Forgiveness

Forgiveness is like a pebble dropped into a pond, creating ripples that spread outward, often unexpectedly affecting other areas of life. Releasing someone from blame can improve our relationships, as we bring less resentment into new connections.

Forgiveness has been demonstrated to benefit mental health, reduce anxiety and depression, and even improve physical health. Chronic resentment has been linked to increased stress, which can harm immune function, heart health, and overall well-being.

By forgiving, we gain emotionally and physically, freeing our bodies and minds from the corrosive effects of unresolved anger. Forgiveness, however, doesn't mean blind trust. While trust requires time and proof of change, forgiveness is about letting go of resentment to create a better present and future. In releasing anger, we let go of the illusion of control over the future, finding peace in accepting life's unpredictability.

One of the most profound examples of forgiveness comes from people who have faced unimaginable loss. Stories of parents forgiving those who caused harm to their children or survivors finding peace with perpetrators demonstrate the incredible strength forgiveness can provide. These acts are not about forgetting or excusing harm but about choosing peace over the pain of prolonged anger. Such forgiveness requires immense courage and a willingness to confront deep emotions, yet it often leads to profound healing and freedom.

If forgiving others is difficult, forgiving ourselves can feel nearly impossible. Often, we judge ourselves more harshly than anyone else, holding onto guilt as if self-punishment could somehow make things right. Yet self-forgiveness is an act of compassion, allowing us to accept our humanity—imperfect, evolving, and capable of change. Self-forgiveness doesn't erase the past but shifts focus to the future, allowing for renewed purpose and self-respect.

By letting go of self-blame, we recognize our capacity for growth, acknowledging our mistakes without letting them define us. Self-forgiveness also involves accepting unmet expectations and past choices made in moments of weakness. But by forgiving ourselves, we embrace our humanity, accepting ourselves with empathy and understanding.

Forgiveness isn't a one-time action; it's an ongoing process that requires patience, self-awareness, and willingness—to forgive ourselves and others. Understanding that hurtful actions often stem from another person's pain or limitations can soften resentment and recognize our shared humanity.

Forgiveness is an inner choice, independent of apologies or validation from others. By releasing expectations, we forgive without waiting for change in others. In many ways, forgiveness becomes an act of self-care, freeing us from relying on others' actions for our peace.

If forgiving someone feels difficult, writing a letter—even if unsent—can clarify feelings and offer closure. Putting thoughts and emotions into words allows for expression, helping to organize overwhelming feelings. This practice provides perspective, freeing us from unresolved hurt.

For example, I was my mother's caretaker for more than a decade before she passed away. Our time together was filled with joyful moments, but sometimes we frustrated each

9 - Echoes of Forgiveness

other, lost patience, and even showed anger. In her final days, as it became clear she was slipping away, I felt overwhelmed with guilt. I questioned whether I had done enough or shown too much frustration. This mixed sadness and gratitude has stayed with me—a paradox of life's journey. That's why I wrote a letter, to make amends not only with her but with myself.

Forgiveness often challenges our ego. The ego, naturally protective, can make forgiveness feel like a threat, as though letting go of resentment compromises our dignity. But a balanced ego helps us forgive from a place of strength rather than vulnerability, allowing forgiveness to flow from self-respect and peace.

Ultimately, forgiveness is a path to inner freedom. By choosing forgiveness, we release ourselves from the actions of others, embracing peace and compassion. This path is not always easy; it requires us to confront pain, acknowledge anger, and let go of the need for retribution. But in doing so, we open ourselves to a life unburdened by past hurts, allowing forgiveness to shape us constructively.

Forgiveness isn't a destination but a way of life, an ongoing choice that creates space for joy, peace, and connection. Living with forgiveness means each day is an opportunity for growth and healing. By forgiving others and ourselves, we compassionately embrace our imperfections, stepping into a future defined by resilience, wisdom, and strength.

In the end, forgiveness transforms our relationships and our entire approach to life. It allows us to move with a lighter heart, unbound by resentment and filled with possibilities guided by understanding, acceptance, and inner freedom.

9 - Echoes of Forgiveness

"Caring for your inner child has a powerful and surprisingly quick result: Do it and the child heals."

– *Martha Beck*

Sexual energy pulses are like a primal force, a power both beautiful and dangerous, capable of creating profound connections or casting shadows of control. It is an energy that can draw us close or divide, a magnetic pull intertwined with desire, identity, and the vulnerabilities we guard. In the delicate balance between attraction and intent, love and lust, lies the potential for manipulation—a force that bends the will, shaping emotions in its wake.

Chapter 10: Sexual Dynamics & Power

Navigating Sexual Power & Manipulation

Reflecting on sexual power and manipulation requires honesty and a willingness to confront personal vulnerability, strengths, and the often subtle boundaries that shape our interactions with others. Through my own experiences, I've learned that the dynamics of attraction, control, and influence can be both empowering and, at times, unsettlingly deceptive.

One of the first things I came to realize was how sexual power is often less about physicality and more about the energy between people. There's an unspoken language in eye contact, body language, and the willingness to step into or shy away from intimacy. For many of us, especially those who've felt a need to prove ourselves or gain a sense of control, sexuality can become a tool—a means of asserting power, gaining attention, or even masking insecurities.

On the other side, manipulation is a shadow that often accompanies sexual power. I've witnessed it, felt it, and, at times, I'm sure, unknowingly wielded it. Manipulation can emerge when one party leverages emotional or physical attraction to elicit a desired response from another. It can be subtle—maybe a hint of seduction to win a favor or a compliment to soften the blow of criticism. Yet, these subtleties can become dangerous in the wrong hands, creating an imbalance of power and leaving scars that linger long after.

Historical Roots

The power one sex has wielded over the other has been deeply shaped by patriarchal systems, positioning men as dominant and women as submissive. For centuries, societal structures have supported men's perceived "ownership" of women's bodies, from marriage laws and property rights to social expectations around chastity and modesty.

These power imbalances have been reinforced through cultural norms and legal systems, often confining women's roles and choices. Feminist movements in the twentieth century challenged these systems, advocating for women's sexual autonomy and fighting against gender-based control. Despite these advances, remnants of patriarchal views on sexuality persist today, sometimes subtly within relationships.

Privilege & Power

As a man writing about sexual power, I feel a particular responsibility to address the role men have historically played in these dynamics. In many instances, men's entitlement to women's bodies has been a cultural norm born out of a patriarchal system and upheld by media and social narratives. This entitlement translates into subtle forms of control that go unnoticed until unpacked.

Recognizing this privilege isn't easy, but it's necessary. Avoiding discomfort only upholds the status quo, preventing meaningful change. Writing about this topic requires me to reflect on past mistakes, face how I may have contributed to these dynamics, and commit to doing better in future relationships.

Abusive Relationships

Abusive relationships often involve a web of control that includes emotional manipulation, verbal attacks, and sometimes physical violence. Over time, these strategies erode self-worth, leaving victims feeling trapped and powerless.

Gaslighting is a particularly damaging form of psychological manipulation in which the abuser causes their partner to question their perceptions, memories, or sense of reality. By denying, minimizing, or twisting the truth, the abuser fosters confusion and self-doubt.

In many abusive relationships, a cycle of mistreatment is punctuated by brief periods of affection, apologies, or even kindness—often referred to as "honeymoon phases." These moments can give the impression that the abuse is temporary or that the relationship is capable of genuine happiness.

Lessons Learned

This chapter isn't written from a place of relationship success but from lessons learned through failure. My experiences have shown how subtle forms of manipulation can seep into intimacy, often unnoticed, until harm is irreparably done. Failures can force us to confront how power operates within our relationships, making us aware of how we might unconsciously influence others.

Responsibility means reflecting on past actions and committing to healthier, more respectful relationships. It requires courage and a willingness to face uncomfortable truths, but it's an essential step toward growth.

Role of Media & Culture

Society plays a significant role in shaping our understanding of sexual power. Media, literature, and legal systems have long reinforced narratives that normalize male dominance and female submission. Movies, books, and TV shows frequently glamorize manipulative behavior, portraying it as romantic or desirable. Recognizing these influences is crucial for breaking free from toxic narratives and building a culture where respect and equality are the norms.

Empowerment & Respect

True empowerment in relationships means recognizing and rejecting manipulation in all its forms. When we unlearn toxic patterns, we open the door to relationships founded on trust, equality, and mutual support. Empowerment doesn't mean striving for dominance; it means creating an environment where both partners feel valued and respected.

Free of Manipulation

Addressing sexual power and manipulation is not a comfortable topic, but it's a necessary one. By examining how power dynamics operate within intimacy, we create the opportunity for change.

We should move beyond traditional roles, challenge assumptions, and create relationships where everyone feels valued and heard. By letting go of manipulation and embracing genuine connection, we pave the way for intimacy that heals, strengthens, and uplifts.

Embracing Life's Journey

When women and men come together, it is a meeting of worlds—each with its rhythms, mysteries, and strengths, weaving a dance as ancient as time. Their connection holds a delicate balance, blending contrasts and harmonies that reflect unity and individuality. In this shared space, there is tension and tenderness, where differences become strengths, and understanding grows not from sameness but from embracing what is distinct.

Chapter 11: Women & Men in Shared Space

I will explore relationship themes and reflections based on my experiences within traditional relationships. While this perspective shapes my insights, I wholeheartedly acknowledge and respect the diversity of relationships, each with its unique dynamics and challenges. This book is written with appreciation for the many forms of love, commitment, and partnership that enrich our world. My reflections are not exhaustive but offered in the spirit of connection, honoring the experiences of all who walk different but equally meaningful paths in their relationships.

Being Together

Sharing life with a partner, friend, or family profoundly transforms us. Being close to someone helps us grow, revealing aspects of ourselves we might never have noticed alone. This relationship becomes a mirror, reflecting our strengths, flaws, and idiosyncrasies while providing companionship and stability through life's unpredictable challenges. Together, we experience joys and hardships, exchanging comfort and support that strengthen our resilience. In building connections, we find purpose and create a legacy of kindness, empathy, and understanding, weaving a tapestry of meaning in our lives.

Evolution of Gender Roles

Historically, men have dominated public and private life, while women were often confined to secondary roles. Movements for women's rights in the nineteenth and twentieth centuries began challenging these norms, advocating for suffrage, education, and workplace inclusion.

Despite significant progress, traditional gender roles still influence perceptions of authority, emotion, and ambition today. Tensions stemming from these dynamics are not inherently negative. While they can lead to misunderstandings and power struggles, they also offer growth opportunities, fostering mutual respect and breaking outdated norms as we move toward equality.

Traditional Roles in Shared Space

In the workplace, traditional roles still impact women's and men's experiences. Women often face challenges like unequal pay and limited leadership opportunities, while men may feel pressured to conform to traditional masculinity. These expectations can create misunderstandings yet also reveal areas where progress is needed. Traditional roles in family and social settings influence relationships,

11 - Women & Men in Shared Space　　　　　　　　　　　　　　88

even as more women enter the workforce and men engage in caregiving. Balancing these evolving roles requires open communication, a willingness to question outdated norms, and mutual support.

The Meaning of Love

Before we become too deeply involved in discussing relationships, I'd like to share my idea about love—both the word and the emotions ascribed to it. It's one of those words we all use, yet it seems like everyone has a slightly different idea of what it truly means. Today, it often feels like our definitions of love are shaped by our individual experiences, backgrounds, and even how we saw love modeled for us growing up. In many ways, men and women were raised to perceive love differently, often influenced by societal expectations and family dynamics.

Falling in Love

I used to think I was smart, and maybe I was—or wasn't. The idea of "falling" in love felt strange for a long time. Head over heels in love? Sure, but what does that mean? And what was the actual falling part all about? Doesn't that hurt? Eventually, as I often do, I came up with a reason for people falling in love.

We fall in love partly because we're on our best behavior when we're "in the market" for a soul mate, consciously or not. It's the same whether we're seeking someone of the same or different gender. We spot a candidate for our ideal partner and start meeting their expectations—intentionally or otherwise. It seems like love, but I think it's meeting each other's expectations.

11 - Women & Men in Shared Space

Conflict & Cooperation

Conflict often arises from rigid expectations of gender roles but can lead to cooperation when approached with openness. By valuing each other's unique strengths, men and women can bridge divides and work toward shared goals. Mutual respect dissolves traditional barriers, fostering collaboration and encouraging inclusive environments where diverse perspectives thrive.

Building Meaningful Connections

Having been in numerous relationships, each one (whether lasting or not) taught me valuable lessons. At the risk of sounding like a textbook marriage counselor, here are a few insights that I believe may contribute to meaningful connections and lasting relationships:

- **Share Thoughts & Feelings**: Open communication builds trust. Sometimes, simply listening is more potent than solving problems.

- **Respect Each Other as Individuals**: Treating each other as unique individuals, rather than adhering to stereotypes, fosters authenticity and growth.

- **Cultivate Empathy**: Empathy allows both partners to share vulnerabilities, fostering trust.

- **Align on Shared Values**: Having shared values strengthens relationships by creating unity and purpose.

- **Support Each Other's Growth**: Encouraging each other's personal and professional goals allows both individuals to thrive.

- **Use Humor to Diffuse Tension**: Humor lightens tense moments, bringing joy and helping both partners approach issues with a lighter heart.

The Path Forward

The journey toward equality is complex, but empathy and understanding can bridge divides. We create partnerships rooted in respect and trust by challenging assumptions and listening to each other's experiences. Empathy allows us to see beyond stereotypes, helping us appreciate each other's unique qualities and dreams.

Culture of Equality

Achieving gender equality requires cultural change, creating spaces where men and women collaborate and respect each other's strengths. This shift involves questioning norms and committing to inclusivity. Equality transcends policy changes and redefined roles. It's about cultivating a collaborative culture where everyone's voice is valued, building a stronger, compassionate, and resilient society. As we move forward, let's embrace empathy, respect, and understanding, crafting a future where both men and women thrive.

11 - Women & Men in Shared Space

"When men and women are able to respect and accept their differences then love has a chance to blossom."
— *John Gray*

Embracing Life's Journey

Solitude is a gentle sanctuary, a quiet embrace where the world's noise falls away, leaving space to hear the soft stirrings of the soul. In this stillness, we find ourselves whole, unfiltered by the presence of others, free to explore the landscapes within. Embracing solitude is not loneliness but a meeting with our truest self, a place where peace settles like morning mist, where creativity awakens, and reflection takes root.

Chapter 12: Embracing Solitude for Inner Peace

In a world that prizes constant connection, solitude is often misunderstood. Many equate being alone with loneliness, but solitude offers a unique space for self-reflection, growth, and healing. It's in these quiet moments that we find clarity and peace. Learning to embrace solitude is an act of self-compassion that builds resilience and self-awareness, helping us become more grounded, centered individuals. Far from fostering isolation, solitude reconnects us with our true selves and strengthens our relationship with the world.

Solitude vs. Isolation

Solitude is frequently mistaken for isolation or withdrawal, but it's not about escaping the world—it's about reconnecting with oneself. While isolation can feel like an absence, solitude is a presence, a time to be with our thoughts and emotions, free from external pressures.

Solitude invites us to slow down and recharge, offering a sanctuary to listen to our inner voice and reflect on what truly matters. This isn't always easy. For some, the idea of solitude can be challenging. My daughter, for instance, has long struggled with being alone. Like my dog, who experiences separation anxiety, she's often restless without company.

I try to remind her that life can be deeply fulfilling without constant companionship. Of course, I'm not trying to compare my daughter to the dog. Personally, I appreciate the peace and satisfaction of being at ease in my own company. In solitude, we step away from others' needs and expectations, allowing our thoughts to settle and our sense of self to become more apparent. In these moments, we become reacquainted with who we are at our core.

After Relationships End

Solitude becomes especially powerful after the end of a relationship. It offers a unique chance for self-discovery and healing, allowing us to process the past without distraction. Taking time alone after a breakup will enable us to reflect on what worked, what didn't, and why.

Without this period of introspection, it's easy to fall into familiar patterns or bring unresolved emotions into future relationships, often leading to similar disappointments.

In the aftermath of a relationship, solitude helps us rediscover our individuality. Personal goals and desires can blur when we're part of a couple, making it essential to reconnect with who we are independently.

Solitude rebuilds confidence and resilience, laying a solid

12 - Embracing Solitude for Inner Peace

foundation for healthier, more balanced relationships in the future. Instead of looking for someone to fill an emotional void, we become more equipped to connect from a place of self-assurance and clarity.

Simplicity in Solitude

The beauty of solitude lies in its simplicity. Solitude doesn't demand productivity, achievement, or validation; it invites us to be still. In this stillness, we can let go of the need to perform, compete, or prove ourselves, allowing our minds and bodies to unwind.

This stillness is not emptiness—it's a fullness of presence that allows us to experience peace simply by being. Quiet moments offer us the space to unwind, reflect, and let our minds and bodies breathe without the outside world's demands.

Solitude encourages us to step back from the noise and look inward. In these moments, we can process our experiences, find insight, and gain perspective on where we're headed.

It's an opportunity to realign our goals, refresh our priorities, and understand ourselves deeper. This pause, however brief, restores our balance and renews our sense of purpose.

Source of Resilience

One of the greatest gifts of solitude is resilience and persistence. Spending time alone teaches us to rely on ourselves for comfort and strength, reducing our dependence on external validation. This self-reliance creates a sturdy foundation that carries us through life's inevitable ups and downs. In solitude, we learn to face our emotions head-on, whether joyous or sorrowful, without needing someone else to carry the burden.

Resilience in solitude also means learning to be comfortable with silence and to sit with our thoughts without feeling the need to fill the void. When we embrace our solitude, we build quiet confidence in our ability to handle whatever life presents. Instead of seeking outside distractions to cope, we turn inward, finding calm within ourselves. This resilience is not about hardening ourselves against the world but cultivating a gentle strength that allows us to gracefully flow through life's challenges.

Self-Discovery

Someone once told me, "Solitude is the birthplace of self-discovery." Alone, we uncover who we are at our core, separate from the influences and expectations of others. Solitude provides the freedom to ask important questions: What makes me happy? What are my passions? Where am I holding myself back?

In solitude, we find clarity about our values and motivations, and this self-awareness empowers us to make choices aligned with our authentic selves. In solitude, we discover our values, dreams, and the areas where we long to grow.

This understanding becomes a guiding compass in our lives, helping us to navigate decisions and relationships with intention. We realize that our lives do not have to be defined by others' expectations but can be shaped by our inner wisdom.

Practicing Solitude

Embracing solitude isn't about avoiding relationships but intentionally making space for oneself. Solitude is a practice that requires regular attention and intention. It might look like setting aside a few quiet moments each day, taking a peaceful walk, journaling, or meditating. These small acts of solitude help us reconnect with ourselves amid the chaos of daily life, building a stronger relationship with our inner world.

Making solitude a regular part of life strengthens our resilience and clarity, helping us handle life's demands more easily. Solitude becomes a sacred time to check in with ourselves, release the day's stresses, and ground ourselves in what truly matters. In solitude, we nurture our well-being, cultivating a calm strength that radiates into all areas of our lives.

Embracing Life's Journey

Solitude of Sleep

Sleep, in its quiet simplicity, is not unlike sitting alone in a chair, surrounded by the stillness of solitude. We retreat to it each night, a pause from the day's demands and a chance to exist in a state of pure being. In sleep, just as in moments of solitude, there is no pressure to perform, interact, or respond. We are simply there resting, recharging, and surrendering to a world where we don't have to think about anything or anyone else.

In sleep, we let go of external expectations and immerse ourselves in a space of complete inner quiet. Dreams add a new layer to this solitude, offering us places that exist only within our minds. Both sleep and dreams offer a freedom that allows us to be—without agendas, analysis, or distractions.

Cultivating Peaceful Solitude

Solitude is a powerful force for growth, resilience, and peace. It's a space where we can be fully ourselves, free from the pressures and expectations of others. Embracing solitude means choosing to know and love ourselves more deeply and building a foundation of self-reliance that enhances every aspect of our lives.

In the end, solitude is not a retreat from life but an invitation to live it more fully. It teaches us that we are enough as we are, reminding us of our strength and our capacity for joy. In solitude, we find a sanctuary within ourselves—a source of endless peace, clarity, and strength that guides us through life's journey.

Embracing Life's Journey

"It is what it is" speaks to life's unchangeable truths, a quiet surrender to what cannot be altered or undone. It is an acceptance as deep as the earth, steadying us in the face of the unknown and inviting us to release our need to control or resist. This phrase carries the wisdom of resilience—a reminder that peace often lies not in fighting reality but in embracing it as it stands.

Chapter 13: Acceptance - It Is What It Is

"It is what it is" has become a common way of expressing acceptance when things are unplanned. From small frustrations to major life challenges, it acknowledges reality without getting trapped in resistance. I used this phrase often after Hurricane Sandy devastated my New Jersey beach home. Sorting through the wreckage, I'd say, "It is what it is." It wasn't just a line but a way of processing what had happened and finding a path forward.

The hurricane destroyed years of work and memories. Standing among the wreckage, I had two choices: resist what had happened or accept it. Saying "It is what it is" wasn't about denying the loss or the pain—it was about acknowledging the reality and focusing on what I could control next. Acceptance didn't mean ignoring the hurt; it meant choosing not to expend energy on what couldn't be undone and directing that energy instead toward what could be rebuilt.

Today, I keep a sign of the expression in my office as a reminder of the power of acceptance. Incidentally, the phrase first appeared in American writing in the 1940s when a rancher described the challenges of farming tough, unforgiving land, saying, "The land is what it is."

This sentiment reflects a long-standing philosophy of acceptance, notably in Stoicism, where thinkers like Marcus Aurelius and Epictetus emphasized that while we cannot control the world around us, we can control our response to it. As Epictetus said, "There is only one way to happiness, and that is to stop worrying about things beyond our control." This is the heart of "It is what it is"—a reminder to let go of what we cannot change and focus on managing what remains.

Acceptance vs. Resignation

There is an essential distinction between acceptance and resignation. Acceptance is active—acknowledging reality and choosing to move forward. Resignation, however, is passive, a feeling of giving up. When we say "It is what it is" from a place of acceptance, we free ourselves from frustration and turn our attention to what we can control. However, when we say it with resignation, the phrase can make us feel powerless and deflated rather than empowered.

Acceptance in Daily Life

We often find ourselves in situations where things don't go according to plan. Maybe it's a job loss, a relationship ending, or an unexpected health issue. In these moments, the inclination to resist is strong. We long to rewrite the past or cling to the way things were. But resistance is exhausting, like swimming upstream against a powerful current. We expend all our energy fighting, only to be frustrated and worn out.

13 - Acceptance - It Is What It Is

Acceptance, by contrast, is like flowing with the current. It allows us to conserve energy and focus on what we can control, moving forward with greater peace. In my life, I've seen people become trapped in anger and bitterness because they resisted change, clinging to what could have been instead of embracing what is. Meanwhile, those who accepted their circumstances, painful though they might be, found a way to move forward calmly and clearly.

Learning from the Stoics

The Stoics often used metaphors to communicate their philosophy, and one metaphor that resonates deeply with me is that of the gardener. As someone who spends hours in my greenhouse, I can relate to the notion that while we can plant and nurture, we cannot control every aspect of growth. The weather, pests, or even unforeseen circumstances may affect the garden, but the gardener accepts this, continuing to nurture what they can.

The approach of "It is what it is" works much the same way. We make plans and invest effort, yet life doesn't always follow our script. Just like a gardener must work with nature's unpredictability, we must also learn to work with life's uncertainties, accepting what is beyond our control while focusing on what we can nurture.

The Stoic view of acceptance doesn't mean passivity or surrender. Rather, it's about cultivating an attitude of resilience, understanding that while we may not control every outcome, we can choose how to respond. Acceptance becomes a tool for emotional freedom, releasing us from the grip of frustration and allowing us to focus on the present moment.

13 - Acceptance - It Is What It Is 106

Accepting Reality

Acceptance doesn't mean inaction. It means understanding what we can't change while choosing to act where we can. After Hurricane Sandy, I accepted the damage but didn't sit in the rubble feeling defeated. I chose to rebuild, taking one step at a time, balancing acceptance with purposeful action. In relationships, work, and personal challenges, this balance is key. Acceptance grounds us, while action propels us forward, helping us to find meaning and purpose in difficult circumstances.

Accepting reality doesn't mean giving up on change. On the contrary, it often gives us a clearer view of the path forward. By facing what we can't alter, we free up mental and emotional space to consider what we can influence. Acceptance doesn't close doors—it opens possibilities, enabling us to act from a place of clarity rather than frustration.

Freedom Not Surrender

At first, "It is what it is" might sound like a surrender phrase, but it's about freedom. It frees us from the relentless pursuit of control, from the stress of trying to force life to fit our expectations. When we embrace "It is what it is," we open ourselves to the present, facing reality directly without the burden of unrealistic hopes or illusions.

This acceptance doesn't mean that we stop hoping or dreaming. It means we cultivate a mindset that can adapt and adjust as life unfolds. We're not locked into one version of happiness or success. Like a gardener nurturing a struggling plant, we don't give up hope—we learn to accept and work with what is, finding beauty and purpose in each stage.

13 - Acceptance - It Is What It Is

Acceptance as a Tool

Getting serious about "It is what it is" brings an inner peace that is hard to achieve when we constantly resist reality. Instead of wasting energy on "what if" or "if only," we focus on the present moment, directing our attention toward what truly matters. This perspective doesn't just bring calm; it also helps us become more resilient and able to handle life's challenges without being overwhelmed.

When we fully accept reality, we are better equipped to deal with whatever comes our way. This mindset can be transformative, enabling us to find peace even in difficult circumstances. Acceptance becomes a compass, guiding us away from bitterness and toward clarity, compassion, and growth.

Life Philosophy

"It is what it is" has grown beyond a catchphrase for me; it's become a way of life. In each challenge, large or small, I remind myself of this truth. Acceptance doesn't eliminate pain or difficulty but changes our relationship with them. Rather than seeing challenges as obstacles, we see them as opportunities to practice resilience and adaptability.

This philosophy of acceptance also teaches us to find contentment in the present. When we're constantly striving to change what is, we overlook the value of what we have. Embracing "It is what it is" helps us appreciate life as it unfolds, finding gratitude in the small moments and meaning in each journey step.

Embracing Life's Journey

Humor is a spark in the dark, a bright thread woven through life's tapestry, softening the sharp edges of our days. It is a reminder not to take ourselves too seriously, to laugh in the face of absurdity, and to find grace in imperfection. In the gift of laughter, we discover resilience, a buoyancy that keeps us afloat when life gets heavy.

Chapter 14: The Power of Humor

Humor is a powerful yet often underrated tool for navigating life's challenges. More than just a way to make people laugh, humor uplifts, connects, and brings much-needed relief in difficult times. It is transformative, serving as a coping mechanism for building resilience, deepening connections, and enriching our lives. During my time as a professional humorist, including an unforgettable night opening for Eddie Murphy in Washington, D.C., I experienced firsthand the impact humor has on people. Strangers were united in laughter, sharing a moment of joy that made everything feel slightly lighter.

Humor can shift our perspective when life gets tough. It allows us to laugh in the face of adversity, a key to resilience. When we see the absurdity in challenging situations, humor gives us the space to detach and reframe. In my life, humor has often been a saving grace, helping me turn my focus from what I couldn't control to how I could respond. Those moments of laughter gave me the strength to keep going, no matter how bleak things seemed.

Deoxyribonucleic Acid

I always thought humor was woven into my family's DNA, or Deoxyribonucleic Acid, as I like to call it. From an early age, laughter was our language, and sharing stories—whether true, exaggerated, or completely absurd—was our way of connecting.

One memory that sticks with me is of interviewing my dad on video about his life memories. He started laughing, and the laughter was contagious. Years later, after he passed, that video became a treasured gem for all of us, a way to feel his presence and laugh alongside him again.

Embracing Life's Journey

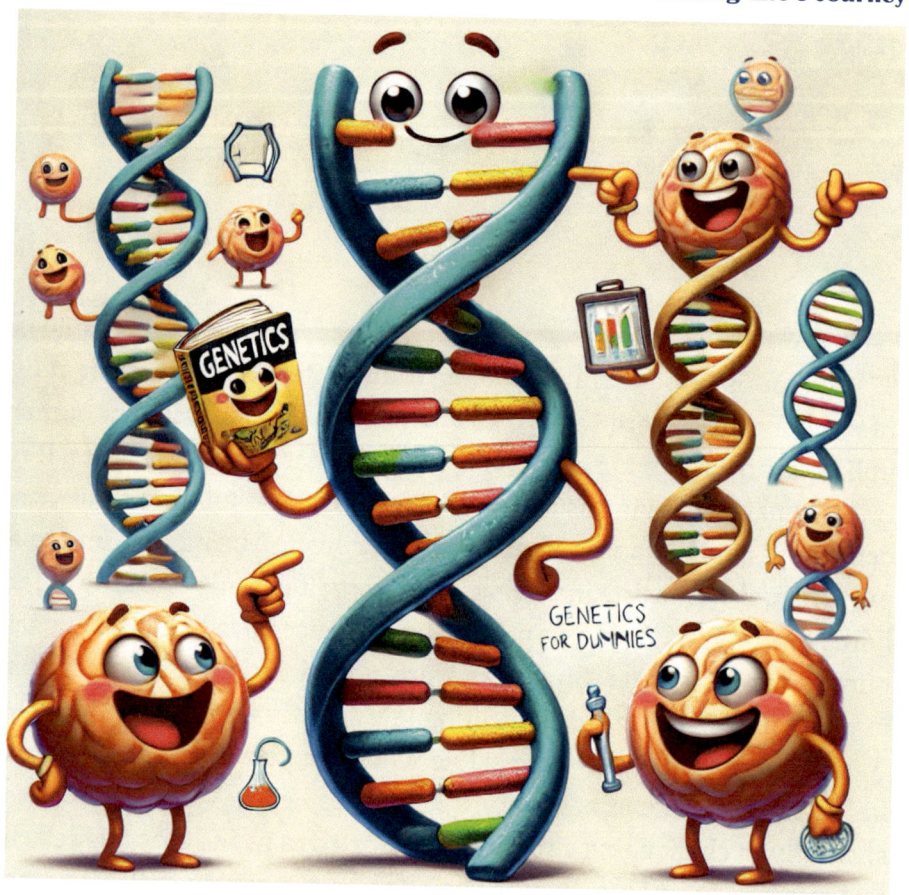

Growing up, humor ran deep in my family. My mom, known for her malapropisms (we called her the "Norm Crosby" of the family), could turn any conversation into a comedy routine. My mom once recounted a night at an Air Force dance, where she yelled, "Who wants my cherry?" after discarding it from her ice cream sundae. I didn't understand why everyone laughed as a kid, but the story stayed with us.

Source of Connection

One of the most remarkable powers of humor is its ability to connect us on a deeper level. A shared laugh can dissolve tension, build rapport, and create bonds that words alone might not. Humor is a universal language that bridges differences and unites people. For example, making a room full of strangers laugh was an incredible experience on stage. The opening for Eddie Murphy was unforgettable,

14 - The Power of Humor   112

not just for the thrill of sharing a stage with him, but because it showed me how laughter could unite a diverse crowd in joy, even if just for a few minutes.

Humor transcends backgrounds, beliefs, and personal histories, allowing us to find common ground through laughter. When we laugh with others, we're saying, "I see you, I understand." It creates an unspoken bond that goes beyond words, fostering a sense of shared experience. Humor brings us together, allowing us to connect with each other's humanity, no matter how different we may seem.

Mirror for Self-Understanding

Humor can serve as a mirror, giving us insight into ourselves. A well-placed joke or a bit of self-deprecation reveals truths about who we are and what we care about. Early in my humorist career, I used comedy to explore relationships, failures, and the absurdities of daily life. Joking about my flaws made me more comfortable, disarming fears that might otherwise weigh me down. By laughing at myself, I could confront and even embrace my imperfections, finding a sense of ease in acknowledging them.

Humor often reveals the unspoken truths of our lives, the quirks and contradictions that make us human. By laughing at these truths, we find acceptance. We recognize that everyone has their flaws, and it's okay to own them. Humor allows us to face the parts of ourselves we might otherwise shy away from, offering a way to approach self-understanding with kindness and curiosity.

Health Benefits

Laughter isn't just good for the soul but has tangible health benefits. Studies show that laughter lowers stress, boosts immunity, and reduces pain by releasing endorphins, the body's natural mood lifters. For me, laughter became a reliable way to reset during difficult

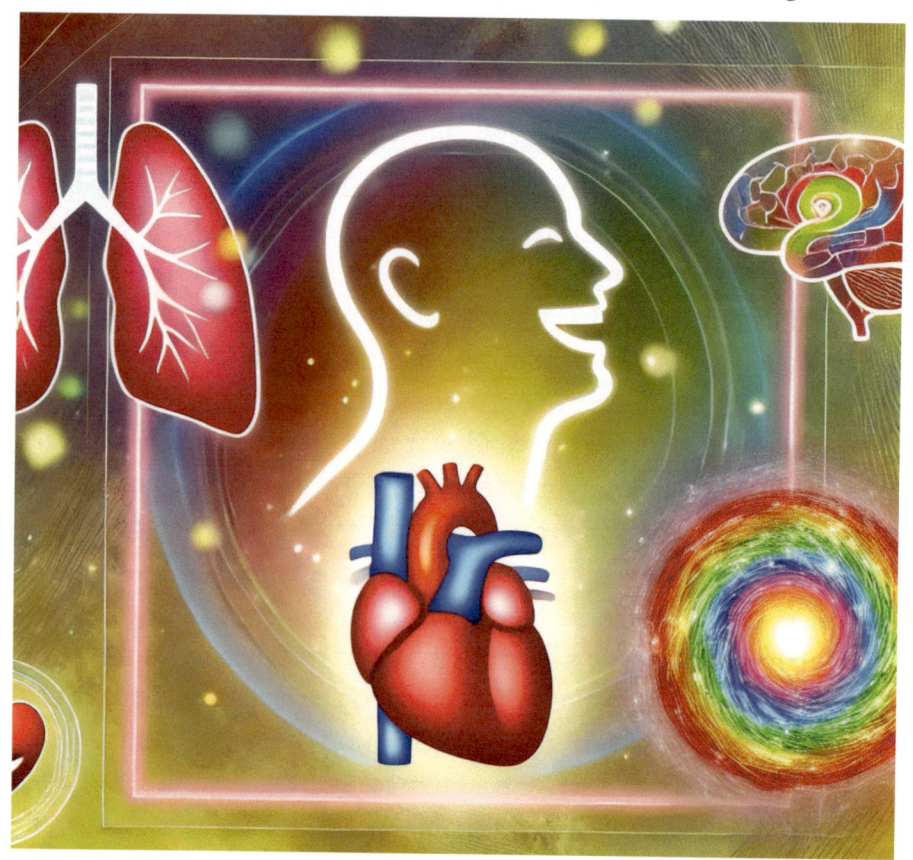

14 - The Power of Humor

times. When we laugh, even briefly, our worries fade, our minds clear, and we regain balance.

Laughter releases tension and invites us to relax, even for a moment. This release is incredibly healing, allowing us to release stress and approach life's challenges with renewed energy. By incorporating humor into our lives, we make life more enjoyable and give ourselves a powerful tool for maintaining well-being. Humor becomes a form of self-care, a way to nurture mind and body.

Coping with Hardship

Humor doesn't ignore pain or difficulty; it helps us face them with dignity and resilience. It's saying, "Yes, this is hard, but I'm still here, and I can still laugh." Humor helped me cope after Hurricane Sandy left my home in disarray. I didn't make light of the loss, but humor allowed me to face it head-on, grounded in who I am. Laughing in the face of adversity wasn't about denying my pain but honoring my resilience.

Life's hardships are inevitable, but humor allows us to meet them gracefully. It acknowledges that even in our darkest moments, there's something to hold onto that can bring us back to ourselves. By finding humor in difficult times, we reclaim a sense of agency, reminding ourselves that we are not defined by our circumstances but by our response to them.

Developing a Sense of Humor

If humor feels out of reach, don't worry; it's a skill that can be nurtured. Humor isn't about becoming a comedian; it's about finding joy in life's absurdities and learning to see things from a lighter perspective. Here are some ways to develop a sense of humor and bring more laughter into your life:

1. Watch stand-up comedy, funny movies, or sitcoms to explore different humor styles.
2. Embrace your quirks and imperfections with humor. Laughing at yourself is incredibly freeing.
3. Focus on the small absurdities of daily life. Mishaps often carry seeds of humor.
4. Spend time with people who make you laugh. Humor is contagious.
5. Cultivate spontaneity and playfulness, always letting go of the need to be serious.
6. Look back on challenges with a lighter heart, imagining how you'll laugh at them later.

By engaging with humor, we make life more enjoyable and create a powerful tool for navigating challenges.

Embracing Life's Journey

Life's dance is a delicate play between control and surrender, each step a balance between holding on and letting go. Control reaches out with steady hands, shaping, guiding, and striving to carve order from chaos. Yet surrender moves with soft grace, releasing, allowing, and trusting the unknown. Together, they form a rhythm—a push and pull where strength meets vulnerability, where purpose flows into acceptance.

Chapter 15: Dance of Control & Surrender

Life balances our urge to control circumstances and our need to surrender to what we cannot change. Society often promotes control to feel secure and accomplish goals, yet letting go brings peace, resilience, and the ability to adapt to life's unpredictability. Finding harmony between these two forces helps us face challenges gracefully, focusing on what truly matters and releasing what doesn't.

Comfort of Control

Control offers the comfort of predictability. Setting goals, making plans, and taking intentional action create a sense of order in our lives, helping us build careers, relationships, and personal achievements. Having control over our environment can feel empowering and satisfying. The ability to plan and achieve offers a framework for growth and self-confidence, reassuring us that our choices and actions have a meaningful impact on our lives.

However, the desire for control can become excessive, leading to stress and frustration when life doesn't follow our carefully designed plans. For example, we might plan a career path, envision the "perfect" relationship, or expect our days to unfold smoothly. But when things don't go as expected, the illusion of control can come crashing down, leaving us feeling lost or disappointed. Life's nature is to change, and when we hold on too tightly to how we think things "should" be, we often suffer more.

What We Cannot Control

The truth is, we can't control other people, time, or fate's twists. Trying to control others can lead to disappointment and strain

Embracing Life's Journey

relationships. When we try to change those around us to fit our expectations, we stifle our growth and theirs, erode trust and connection, and build unhealthy relationships. Respecting others' autonomy while focusing on our responses is key to building healthy relationships and a stable inner life.

The dance between control and surrender begins with recognizing these limits and accepting that some things are beyond our reach. This acceptance doesn't mean giving up; it means being wise enough to know when to act and when to let things be. As the familiar Serenity Prayer suggests: "Grant me the serenity to accept the things I cannot change, the courage to change the things I can, and the wisdom to know the difference."

Control & Surrender

Control and surrender may seem like opposites, yet they are partners. Together, they create a balanced approach to life, where we act purposefully but remain open to change. Imagine control and

15 - Dance of Control & Surrender

surrender as partners in a dance. Each has its moment to lead, but the dance only works when there is a mutual give and take.

Control helps us set goals and pursue them with determination. It encourages us to take responsibility for our actions and strive for improvement. Surrender allows us to release attachment to specific outcomes, embracing life's twists and turns without resistance. This blend builds resilience, enabling us to adapt to change while staying aligned with our values and purpose.

The Role of Disintegration

Here, I want to introduce a concept that has helped me understand the interplay of control and surrender more deeply: disintegration.

Embracing Life's Journey

Disintegration is the process by which something falls apart, whether it's a plan, a relationship, or even an aspect of our identity. While this might sound negative, it's often a necessary part of growth.

Disintegration allows us to see where things no longer serve us—where old habits, beliefs, or structures need to be broken down to make room for something new. It teaches us to embrace the temporary chaos that often precedes clarity and transformation.

When we cling too tightly to control, we resist disintegration, fearing the loss of stability. But surrendering to disintegration doesn't mean giving up—it means trusting the change process and allowing things to fall apart when necessary so they can come back together in a healthier, more aligned way.

15 - Dance of Control & Surrender

Dangers of Over-Control

When the need for control becomes overwhelming, we may resort to manipulation or rigid thinking to achieve our desired outcomes. We may try to force situations or people into compliance, feeling that we alone know what's best. This approach, however, provides only temporary security, ultimately damaging trust and authenticity in relationships.

Seeking to control everything can also drain our energy. The constant vigilance required to manage life leaves little room for spontaneity or joy. We miss life's unexpected gifts when we insist on steering every detail. True peace comes not from controlling others but from respecting their autonomy and focusing on our choices. Recognizing the dangers of over-control allows us to adopt a more balanced, constructive approach that values intention and openness.

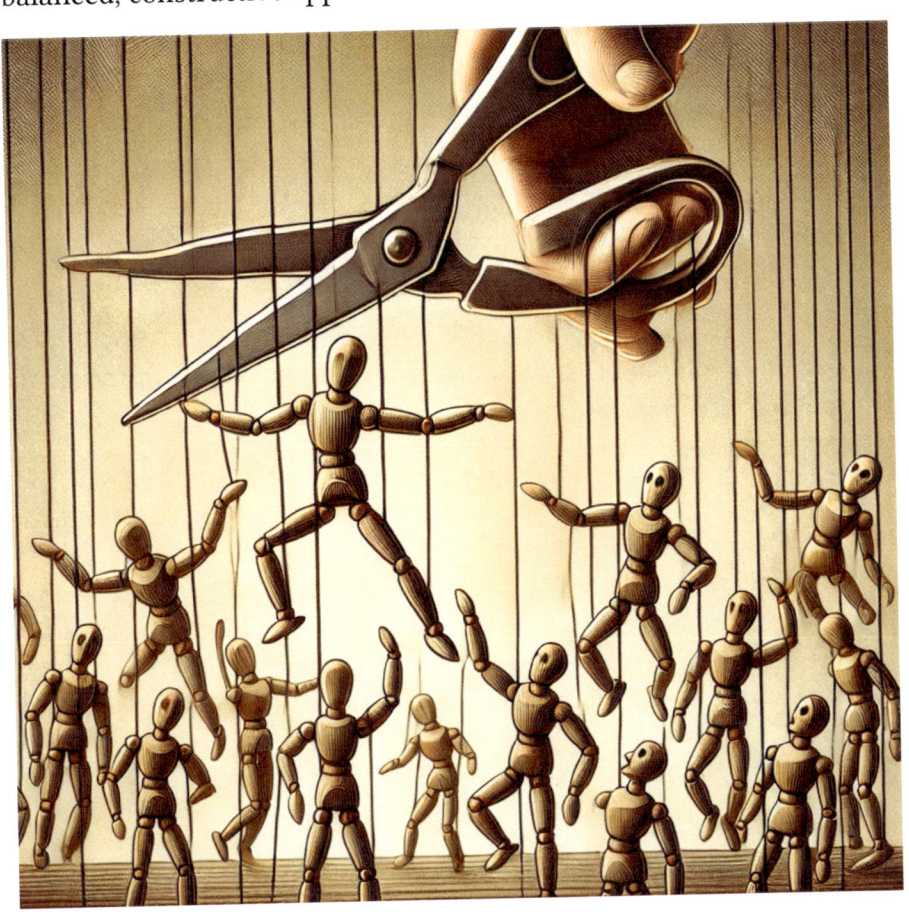

Letting Go

Letting go of control is not an act of resignation but one of liberation. Surrender allows us to release unrealistic expectations, pursue our goals joyfully, and free ourselves from the pressure of making everything "right." This freedom brings a profound sense of peace, enabling us to live fully and appreciate life's serendipitous moments.

Surrender also helps us let go of the need for others' validation. We stop trying to shape ourselves to meet external expectations and begin to honor our path. Letting go empowers us to live authentically, building self-confidence and inner peace. We find space for creativity, spontaneity, and joy by releasing our grip on perfection and control.

The Gift of Balance

One of the greatest gifts of balancing control and surrender is resilience. Life is unpredictable, and challenges are inevitable. The balance between control and surrender helps us approach difficulties gracefully, allowing us to respond thoughtfully rather than out of fear. In times of uncertainty, we rely on our adaptability, trusting that we have the tools and inner strength to face whatever comes our way.

Resilience doesn't mean avoiding hardship; it means growing through it. Control helps us face challenges head-on, while surrender reminds us to accept what we cannot change. Together, these qualities provide a foundation of strength, enabling us to navigate life's storms without losing ourselves.

Steps for Practicing the Dance

1. **Set Intentions Without Attachment**: Establish clear goals but avoid tying your self-worth to specific outcomes.
2. **Focus on What You Can Control**: Direct your energy toward your thoughts, actions, and reactions.
3. **Stay Present**: Surrender brings us back to what is happening now.
4. **Develop Trust**: Believe that each experience contributes to your growth.
5. **Embrace Imperfection**: Free yourself to experience life with curiosity and wonder.
6. **Reflect Regularly**: Learn from successes and setbacks to guide future actions.

The dance of control and surrender is a lifelong practice that teaches us to navigate life with flexibility, grace, and wisdom. Embracing this balance allows us to move through life's challenges with resilience and joy, trusting the rhythm of change while shaping our path forward.

Embracing Life's Journey

Obstacles rise like stones on our path, each a silent test, a challenge calling us to grow stronger, wiser, and more resilient. Moving through them is an art, a blend of patience, courage, and the ability to see beyond the immediate struggle. Each step teaches us to bend without breaking, adapt, and find new routes when the old ones are blocked. These barriers become stepping stones, shaping and revealing our journey.

Chapter 16: Moving Through Obstacles

Albert Einstein said, "The only source of knowledge is experience." This quote captures a core truth about life: challenges refine us and teach us invaluable lessons that we can't learn any other way. Obstacles may never truly disappear, but each one equips us with wisdom and resilience, making it easier to face whatever comes next. Through experience, we gather the tools and strength needed to move through new challenges more clearly and calmly.

Evolution of Resolution

Obstacles may change, but our ability to handle them evolves. The first major setback in life often feels overwhelming, an insurmountable wall that blocks our path forward. Yet, as we gain experience, we find that what once seemed insurmountable becomes manageable. Looking back, we see that each challenge we've overcome has added to our inner toolkit, giving us the confidence to tackle new obstacles. When a fresh hurdle arises, it helps to remember what we've already faced and overcome. Chances are, we're stronger and more resolved than we think.

Persistence is one of the greatest gifts experiences bring us. It's the strength to recover and keep going, no matter how difficult the journey may seem. Early setbacks can feel crushing, yet we build emotional endurance each time we bounce back. Persistence doesn't eliminate discouragement or frustration, but it empowers us to keep going, growing stronger each time we pick ourselves up. In this way, persistence is less about avoiding hardship and more about embracing the process of moving through it.

Embracing Imperfection

In youth, we often strive for perfection, fearing failure and judgment. We place immense pressure on ourselves to get everything right, to be flawless. But life soon shows us that growth, not perfection, is the real goal. Perfectionism can paralyze us from taking risks that lead to growth. Realizing that mistakes are part of the journey helps us approach obstacles with a more open and forgiving mindset that allows for trial, error, and discovery without expecting flawless outcomes.

With experience comes perspective. In hindsight, what once felt like a monumental setback becomes a small chapter in a much larger story. Our mistakes and setbacks don't define us; they are simply part of our journey. This shift in perspective allows us to approach each new challenge with a broader view, seeing it as temporary rather than all-consuming. Each obstacle becomes part of the learning process rather than a defining event.

Value of Patience

With time and experience, we learn that not every problem requires an immediate fix. Experience teaches us patience, the understanding that some solutions reveal themselves over time. In our early years, it's natural to feel a sense of urgency, to want every problem solved right now. But rushing often complicates things, creating unnecessary stress and hindering us from seeing the bigger picture. Patience allows us to trust the process, knowing that some challenges resolve themselves as we gain insight and clarity over time.

Patience isn't passive; it's an active acceptance of the flow of life, an understanding that forcing solutions can sometimes lead to unintended consequences. Patience teaches us to remain calm and observe, allowing life to unfold as it will. This calm confidence allows us to move through obstacles with greater ease, trusting that we'll find the answers we need as we go.

Personal Toolkit

As we navigate life's challenges, we develop a personal toolkit—strategies, insights, and support systems that grow with each experience. This toolkit includes practical skills and emotional resources, such as self-compassion, persistence, and adaptability. Over time, we learn what works best for us in times of stress, what helps us stay grounded, and what resources to call upon when things get tough.

Our toolkit might include trusted friends or mentors, mindfulness practices, problem-solving techniques, or simple routines that keep us centered. Each experience teaches us more about what we need to thrive. One of the most valuable lessons we learned is that sometimes, the best solution is to reach out for help. Asking for support doesn't make us weak; it's a sign of strength, a recognition that we're not alone in our journey.

Learning Through Failure

Failure, though painful, is one of life's most powerful teachers. Each setback refines our approach, making us more adaptable and open to new ways of thinking. Instead of fearing failure, experience shows us that each stumble brings us closer to success. Failure becomes less of an end and more of another step, a chance to learn, adapt, and grow.

Power of Adaptability

Life constantly throws us new challenges, each with unique difficulties. Experience fosters flexibility, helping us think creatively and explore solutions we might not have considered before. When we become more adaptable, we learn to trust that we will find our way forward, no matter how complex the challenge.

Growth Opportunities

Obstacles aren't just problems to be solved; they're growth opportunities. Each challenge we face strengthens and refines us, preparing us for what lies ahead. Over time, obstacles become less intimidating because we trust our ability to move through them.

Strategies for Moving Through

- Break It Down: Tackle challenges in manageable steps.
- Practice Flexibility: Adjust your approach as needed.
- Celebrate Progress: Small victories matter.
- Lean on Support: Ask for help when needed.

Obstacles become stepping stones, not roadblocks. Moving through them shapes who we are, turning challenges into opportunities for transformation.

16 - Moving Through Obstacles

Every obstacle you overcome is a step closer to your dreams. They are not walls meant to stop you, but challenges meant to strengthen you, to test your resolve, and to teach you what you're truly capable of. The path to greatness is paved with perseverance, and every setback is an opportunity to rise again, stronger and wiser.
– *Ralph Waldo Emerson*

Identity flows like a river, ever-shifting, shaped by each bend, each current of experience, never quite the same from one moment to the next. We are both the roots of where we began and the branches reaching toward where we're going, transformed by every encounter and every choice.

Chapter 17: Identity in Flux

Identity often feels like the bedrock of who we are, defined by names, careers, relationships, and values. We grow up hearing phrases like "be true to yourself" or "find your true calling," which suggest that identity is a singular, fixed essence. Yet, identity is anything but fixed. It's a fluid, evolving journey shaped by each experience, phase, and challenge.

Comfort in Stability, Danger in Rigidity

We often cling to the idea of a fixed identity, a stable core that provides comfort and familiarity. Knowing ourselves in certain ways—our likes, dislikes, values, and beliefs—gives us a sense of direction and purpose. However, holding too tightly to a fixed sense of self can be limiting, especially when life's natural changes push us to evolve. When we cling to outdated versions of ourselves, we risk staying trapped in patterns that no longer serve us and feeling lost as the world shifts.

Identity as a fixed concept feels comforting because it provides predictability, but life rarely follows such linear paths. Experiences constantly reshape us, sometimes in ways we couldn't anticipate. Looking back, we see how changes, even unplanned ones, expand our understanding of ourselves. Growth doesn't mean losing who we are; it means deepening and broadening what we know about ourselves.

Inner- vs. Outer-Directed Living

In college, I encountered a concept that reshaped my understanding of identity: inner-directed versus outer-directed living. Inner-directed people make choices based on personal values, while outer-directed individuals are guided more by external validation and societal

Embracing Life's Journey

expectations. Realizing that much of my life was outer-directed was eye-opening. I often let the opinions of others influence my actions, even when they conflict with my values. Over time, I've worked to find a balance, aligning my actions more closely with my inner compass while staying connected to others.

This balance is not static—it requires continual adjustment. Life's circumstances often tip the scales one way or the other, but mindfulness helps us correct course. The goal is to remain true to ourselves while embracing how others enrich our journey.

Lessons from Stories and Film

Some films and stories beautifully illustrate the fluidity of identity, showing how small moments or choices can lead to profound shifts. For instance, Run Lola Run demonstrates how repeating the same time frame with different choices leads the protagonist to vastly different outcomes. Her identity evolves with each attempt, proving that setbacks shape us as much as successes.

Similarly, Sliding Doors explores how missing a single train creates two diverging life paths, each revealing a different version of the protagonist. These stories remind us that our identities are not fixed destinies but living, breathing mosaics shaped by our decisions, challenges, and circumstances.

Phases of Identity

Identity isn't built all at once; it unfolds in layers over time. Childhood, adolescence, adulthood, and later life bring unique challenges and revelations. Childhood often roots us in familial and cultural norms. Adolescence tests those norms as we seek independence. Adulthood reshapes us through responsibilities, relationships, and self-reflection. Later life can deepen our perspective, offering clarity on what truly matters.

Accepting that identity evolves allows us to embrace change without fear. Each phase invites us to redefine ourselves, shedding outdated layers and welcoming new dimensions of our identity.

The Trap of Labels

Labels, such as parent, artist, leader, and caretaker, can help define aspects of ourselves, but they're also temporary. Relying too heavily on labels can limit us, especially when life circumstances shift. For example, someone identifying primarily as a parent might struggle to redefine themselves once their children leave home. Embracing a more fluid sense of self helps us navigate these transitions without losing sight of our core identity.

Similarly, relationships can shape our sense of self, revealing qualities we didn't know we had. While relationships are invaluable, they shouldn't be our sole source of identity. When relationships end or change, we need a stable sense of self to carry us forward.

Navigating Transitions

Life's transitions—career changes, personal losses, new relationships—can feel like identity's most disorienting moments. Yet, these periods of flux are also opportunities for profound growth. Transitions force us to reevaluate what matters most, shedding aspects of ourselves that no longer fit and making space for new possibilities.

In these moments, curiosity and openness are essential. Instead of fearing change, we can ask ourselves: What is this transition teaching me? What am I letting go of, and what am I gaining? By reframing transitions as opportunities for self-discovery, we can navigate them with greater resilience and grace.

Strategies for Embracing Identity in Flux

- Reflect Regularly: Journaling, meditation, or quiet reflection helps clarify who you are and where you're headed.
- Stay Curious: Approach life with a beginner's mind, open to new experiences and perspectives.
- Release Old Labels: Let go of roles or identities that no longer serve you.
- Accept Uncertainty: Embrace change as a natural part of life.
- Focus on Core Values: Anchor yourself in consistent principles, even as other aspects of your identity shift.
- Celebrate Growth: Acknowledge small victories as you evolve.

Identity as a Journey

Identity is not a fixed point but an unfolding narrative. Each experience, challenge, and triumph adds depth to our story, shaping who we are and can become. Accepting this fluidity allows us to approach life with curiosity and compassion, finding beauty in the process of becoming.

Rather than fear change, we can embrace it, trusting that each phase of life brings us closer to understanding our true selves. Identity, like life, is a journey of discovery—a mosaic of moments, connections, and choices that together form the ever-evolving masterpiece of who we are.

17 - Identity in Flux

"To be yourself in a world that is constantly trying to make you something else is the greatest accomplishment."
— *Ralph Waldo Emerson*

Embracing Life's Journey

Purpose beckons us toward meaning, yet in pursuing it, we find ourselves in a dance of questions and contradictions, caught between the desire to achieve and the need to be. In this paradox, we learn that purpose is not a single path but the weaving of many—a constant discovery of how our lives touch the world.

Chapter 18: Paradox of Purpose

The pursuit of purpose is one of life's great quests. We search for meaning in careers, relationships, and personal growth, hoping to find a guiding force that anchors our existence. A clear sense of purpose offers direction and belonging, motivating us to persevere through challenges. Yet this quest is often fraught with contradictions, as seeking purpose can obscure its presence in our lives.

When we view purpose rigidly, believing it is a fixed, ultimate endpoint, we risk creating unnecessary pressure and dissatisfaction. Conversely, when we approach it with curiosity and openness, we find that purpose evolves alongside us, expanding to meet the changing contours of our lives. The purpose isn't a singular truth but a mosaic of experiences, relationships, and quiet moments that together form a meaningful existence.

Illusion of a Singular Purpose

Many of us are taught to see purpose as a grand, singular calling—a career, achievement, or legacy that defines us. While this perspective can inspire ambition, it also creates the illusion that there is only one "right" purpose. This belief can lead to frustration when life doesn't align neatly with our expectations or when we feel uncertain about our path.

In truth, purpose is multifaceted. It can be found in diverse areas of our lives—from the care we provide to loved ones to fulfilling personal goals. These overlapping purposes create a rich tapestry where small, meaningful actions hold as much weight as significant accomplishments. By embracing this broader view, we free ourselves from the pressure to identify a single, all-encompassing purpose and instead focus on cultivating a life full of purpose-filled moments.

Purpose in Everyday Moments

Purpose doesn't have to be monumental. It often reveals how we might help a friend, teach a child, or be present for someone in need. These moments of connection and care, though unassuming, carry immense meaning. For instance, the joy of sharing a laugh with a loved one or supporting a colleague in a time of need can hold as much purpose as achieving a long-term goal. Recognizing the value of these small moments allows us to see how deeply purpose is embedded in daily life. When we pause to appreciate these experiences, we realize that purpose isn't something to be found "out there." It's already present, woven into the fabric of our everyday lives.

18 - Paradox of Purpose

The Paradox of Achievement

Achievement is often equated with purpose but can also be a source of paradox. On one hand, striving for goals gives our lives structure and meaning. On the other hand, tying our sense of purpose too closely to achievement can lead to feelings of emptiness once the goal is reached. True purpose lies in the outcome and the process—the growth, learning, and connections we experience. By redefining success as alignment with our values rather than external validation, we shift our focus from what we achieve to how we live. This perspective encourages us to appreciate the journey, finding fulfillment in each step rather than waiting for a destination to bring meaning.

Curiosity: The Key to Purpose

Curiosity is a powerful ally in the search for purpose. It opens the door to exploration, encouraging us to ask questions, try new things, and embrace the unknown. Instead of viewing purpose as a rigid goal, curiosity allows us to see it as a dynamic process that evolves as we grow. We experiment with different paths, interests, and passions by staying curious. This flexibility helps us adapt when life takes unexpected turns, allowing purpose to emerge naturally rather than being forced. Curiosity keeps us engaged with life, transforming the search for purpose into an ongoing adventure.

Purpose Across Life's Phases

Purpose is not static; it shifts and grows with us through life's phases. What feels meaningful in one stage may change as our priorities and circumstances evolve.

In our early years, purpose often centers on exploration—discovering our talents, building relationships, and setting the foundation for our future.

In midlife, the purpose may shift toward family, career, or community contributions, reflecting our desire for stability and impact.

As we age, purpose often becomes more reflective, focusing on legacy, mentorship, and the pursuit of inner peace.

By embracing this fluidity, we allow ourselves to redefine purpose as we grow, ensuring it remains authentic and fulfilling throughout our lives.

Balancing Being & Doing

The paradox of purpose often lies in balancing the drive to achieve with the need to simply be. In a world that prizes productivity, it's easy to equate purpose with constant doing. Yet some of life's most profound moments come from stillness, reflection, and presence. Purpose isn't just about what we accomplish; it's about who we are. By taking time to pause, reflect, and connect with ourselves and others, we cultivate a more profound sense of purpose that transcends external measures of success.

Strategies for Finding Purpose

- **Reflect on Values**: Spend time identifying what truly matters to you. These values serve as a compass, guiding your decisions and actions.
- **Embrace Small Moments**: Notice the meaning in everyday interactions and tasks. Purpose often hides in the details.
- **Stay Open to Change**: Allow your sense of purpose to evolve as you grow and encounter new experiences.
- **Follow Curiosity**: Pursue interests that spark joy and wonder, even if they don't fit a traditional purpose mold.
- **Practice Gratitude**: Recognize and appreciate the purpose already present in your life.

Living the Paradox

The purpose is not a destination but a journey—a dance between striving and being, between certainty and curiosity. It's found in the grand gestures and the quiet moments, in the questions we ask and the answers we uncover. By embracing the paradox of purpose, we open ourselves to a richer, more meaningful life. We learn to find purpose not in reaching a single endpoint but in weaving together the threads of our experiences, relationships, and personal growth into a tapestry of meaning. This perspective frees us to live fully, confident that purpose is not something we must chase but something we create with each moment we embrace.

18 - Paradox of Purpose

"We are all connected. To each other, biologically. To the earth, chemically. To the rest of the universe, atomically. The fabric of life is woven with threads of interconnection, and every choice we make ripples through the web of existence."

– Neil deGrasse Tyson

Embracing Life's Journey

Visualization is the mind's canvas, where dreams take shape, hope colors the edges of possibility, and belief breathes life into vision. Positive thinking is the light that fills this landscape, shifting shadows and illuminating paths yet to be walked. Together, they are a powerful alchemy, turning desire into intention and action.

Chapter 19: Harnessing the Mind

Our thoughts shape how we experience the world, and visualization and positive thinking are powerful tools for personal growth. By cultivating a clear vision of the life we want and maintaining an optimistic outlook, we can influence our mindset and, in turn, our actions and outcomes.

Visualization and positive thinking empower us to overcome challenges, stay resilient, and align with our aspirations. These practices help us develop an internal compass that directs us toward fulfilling our deepest goals, enhancing our lives, and how we engage with the world around us.

The Science Behind Visualization

Visualization is creating vivid mental images of our goals, mentally rehearsing specific outcomes, and imagining ourselves as we wish to be. Neuroscience shows that the brain responds to these imagined experiences as if they were real. When we visualize ourselves succeeding or overcoming challenges, we activate neural pathways that strengthen over time, which helps us act confidently and effectively when the moment comes. This process is similar to physical practice—visualizing success "exercises" the brain, making it more prepared and responsive when encountering real-life situations.

This technique is widely used in sports, medicine, and performance. Athletes, for example, often visualize completing routines, scoring plays, or crossing the finish line. This mental rehearsal doesn't just improve physical performance; it builds confidence and primes the brain for success. Likewise, musicians and public speakers often visualize performing successfully to reduce anxiety and boost confidence.

Visualization isn't reserved for high-stakes performance—it's a practice anyone can use to reinforce positive behaviors, reduce self-doubt and develop an empowered mindset.

Old Identities

Imagination is the gateway to possibilities, allowing us to envision lives, qualities, and achievements we haven't yet realized. By dreaming or imagining ourselves as successful, resilient, or fulfilled, we "train" the subconscious mind to accept these traits as part of our reality. Over time, the brain begins to adopt these positive traits as familiar, comfortable states, helping to align our conscious actions with the qualities we aspire to embody.

Dreams tap into our subconscious mind, creating experiences that

19 - Harnessing the Mind   150

feel real and are perceived by the brain as such. By visualizing ourselves with the confidence and success we desire, the brain adopts these traits as familiar, gradually reducing resistance to change. Visualization allows us to rehearse different aspects of our lives, from how we wish to communicate to how we want to handle challenges, offering our subconscious a preview of the life we aspire to create.

Mindset for Growth

Positive thinking is often misunderstood as merely "looking on the bright side," but it's much more profound. Positive thinking isn't about ignoring difficulties but choosing a perspective that focuses on solutions, growth, and resilience. We're more likely to respond constructively to challenges when approaching situations with a positive mindset. This optimistic outlook helps reshape our perception of setbacks, helping us see them as opportunities for growth rather than insurmountable roadblocks.

Research has shown that optimism has tangible benefits for our health and well-being. Optimistic individuals experience lower stress levels, better problem-solving skills, and improved health outcomes. Studies suggest positive thinking can strengthen the immune system, reduce the risk of chronic diseases, and promote longevity. By focusing on the positive aspects of our lives, we cultivate resilience, equipping ourselves to bounce back from adversity with greater ease.

Visualization & Positive Thinking as Partners

Visualization and positive thinking are deeply intertwined, amplifying the other's effectiveness. Visualization creates the mental blueprint, while positive thinking fuels the emotional energy that brings that vision to life. Together, they form a powerful practice that enables us to approach life's challenges confidently and intentionally. When we consistently envision ourselves achieving our goals and approach challenges with optimism, we reinforce our belief in our potential, making it easier to take inspired action.

A combination of visualization and positive thinking helps us respond to life with resilience and determination. For example, visualizing success can boost confidence and clarity when facing a difficult project or situation. By approaching the challenge with a positive mindset, we create an internal dialogue that supports our actions, reminding us that we are capable and resilient. This partnership between visualization and positive thinking is a proactive approach to self-development, helping us build a foundation of self-belief that propels us toward our goals.

Creating a Bucket List

A bucket list is more than a list of desires—it's a roadmap for intentional living, encouraging us to prioritize meaningful experiences. As we grow, our understanding of time limits sharpens, prompting us to consider what truly matters. Creating a bucket list is

19 - Harnessing the Mind   152

a powerful visualization exercise, allowing us to clarify our values and aspirations and align them with actionable goals. This list is a tangible representation of our dreams and intentions, reminding us to live in a way that's true to our inner desires.

Bucket lists don't have to focus solely on big adventures or extravagant achievements—they can include personal milestones, creative pursuits, or steps toward emotional healing. A bucket list can be as simple as learning a new skill, connecting with a loved one, or setting aside time for self-care. By revisiting our list over time, we learn the value of adaptability, understanding that our goals may evolve as we do. The journey toward each item often brings as much satisfaction as completing it, reminding us that fulfillment comes from growth and experiences, not just checked boxes.

Everyday Life

Visualization and positive thinking are not limited to specific goals or extraordinary moments; they can be applied to daily life in countless ways. Visualizing a productive day, a meaningful conversation, or a calm response to stress can have a powerful impact on our daily experience. Each small step toward incorporating these practices strengthens our ability to approach life intentionally and confidently.

Consider visualizing your morning routine as a calming, centered experience. This simple practice can set a positive tone for the day, helping you approach each task. Or visualize yourself handling a challenging situation at work with grace and composure, picturing the desired outcome. Even seemingly small moments, visualization, and positive thinking empower us to create a more intentional, fulfilling day.

Positive thinking in daily life means choosing gratitude, focusing on solutions, and reminding ourselves of our strengths. It involves reframing negative or limiting thoughts and replacing them with constructive, empowering messages. This consistent practice gradually rewires our brains, helping us build resilience and develop a more optimistic perspective.

19 - Harnessing the Mind

Techniques for Practicing

- **Create a Vision Board:** A vision board is a powerful tool for visualizing your goals. It gathers images, quotes, and symbols that represent your aspirations. Creating and regularly viewing your vision board reinforces your goals and keeps you focused on what you want to achieve.
- **Daily Visualization Practice**: Set aside a few minutes daily to visualize your goals. Picture yourself achieving them with as much detail as possible. Engage all your senses—see, hear, and feel the experience as if it were happening now. This mental rehearsal strengthens your commitment to your goals.
- **Affirmations for Positive Thinking**: Affirmations are positive statements that help counter self-doubt and negative thinking. Repeating affirmations daily reinforces empowering beliefs and cultivates a positive mindset. Examples include "I am capable of achieving my goals" or "I handle challenges with confidence and resilience."
- **Focus on Small Wins**: Break down significant goals into smaller steps and celebrate each accomplishment. Recognizing progress boosts confidence and encourages a positive mindset, helping you maintain momentum toward your bigger vision.
- **Practice Gratitude**: Gratitude is a cornerstone of positive thinking. By focusing on what you're grateful for each day, you shift your perspective toward abundance rather than lack, fostering a mindset of positivity and contentment.
- **Visualize Overcoming Obstacles**: Visualization isn't just about seeing the end goal—it's about mentally rehearsing how you'll navigate challenges along the way. By visualizing yourself handling obstacles with resilience and composure, you prepare yourself to face real-life setbacks confidently.

Combined with intentional living, visualization and positive thinking offer tools to create a fulfilling and meaningful life. By imagining the person we wish to be and cultivating an optimistic outlook, we take steps toward realizing our goals, embracing the journey along the way. Visualization helps clarify what we want, while positive thinking fuels the motivation to pursue it, empowering us to live in alignment with our true aspirations.

Visualization and positive thinking encourage us to live with intention, making choices that reflect our values and goals. Rather than being reactive, we approach life proactively, guided by a vision of who we wish to become. This approach fosters a sense of agency and fulfillment, reminding us that we can shape our experiences, even when external circumstances are beyond our control.

19 - Harnessing the Mind

Embracing the Power Within

Visualization and positive thinking are transformative practices that allow us to tap into our potential, setting a foundation for a life filled with purpose and joy. They are more than just techniques—they are mindsets that encourage us to see possibilities, dream boldly, and believe in our power to create change. By cultivating a clear vision and nurturing a positive perspective, we build resilience, self-confidence, and the courage to pursue our dreams.

Living intentionally through visualization and positive thinking is a commitment to our growth that celebrates both the journey and the destination. As we harness these practices, we become active participants in our lives, shaping our reality with purpose, optimism, and joy. In this way, we turn dreams into reality, guided by the strength of our imagination and the light of positive thought.

Embracing Life's Journey

Resilience is the art of rising when life has knocked us down, a quiet strength that shapes our character and fortifies our spirit. Through resilience, we transform struggles into stepping stones, weaving a legacy that speaks not just of survival but of purpose and impact. Our legacy echoes our actions, the story we leave behind, and the light that guides others long after we're gone. Together, resilience and legacy define the essence of a life well-lived—a testament to the courage, kindness, and determination that make us human.

Chapter 20: Embracing Resilience & Crafting a Legacy

Life's challenges often feel insurmountable, don't they? The kind that leaves us wondering how we'll find the strength to move forward. But what if these challenges are the threads that weave the fabric of who we are? Resilience is not just about bouncing back—it's about adapting, growing, and transforming. And our legacy? That's the tapestry we create, one thread at a time, from the life we've lived and the lessons we've learned.

Resilience isn't something we're born with—it's something we build, layer by layer, through experiences. Think about a time you faced hardship. Maybe it was losing a job, enduring heartbreak, or coping with illness. Did you notice how, over time, you found a way to adapt? Resilience grows in small moments: when you get out of bed on a tough day when you admit you need help when you find a way to laugh even as you cry.

It's not about being unshakable—it's about learning to sway with life's winds without breaking. The Japanese concept of *kintsugi*, repairing broken pottery with gold, reminds us that our scars make us more beautiful, not less.

It's easy to feel overwhelmed, but resilience starts with how we frame the problem. Instead of seeing a roadblock, ask, "What can this teach me?" Sure, it might sound cliché, but this shift can transform despair into determination. Amid the chaos, mindfulness is your anchor. Take a deep breath. Right now, you're okay. Use this as a foundation to take the next step, however small.

We often feel like we must go it alone, but that's untrue. Resilience doesn't mean isolation. It's calling a friend, seeking advice, or even sharing a meal with someone who cares. Failure stings, but every misstep is a teacher. The next time you falter, ask yourself, "What can I do differently?" Resilience isn't about avoiding failure but mastering the art of starting again.

Now, let's shift gears. Resilience is deeply personal, but our legacy? That's where our lives ripple outward, touching others in ways we may never fully know. Think of your legacy as the story you're writing

20 - Embracing Resilience & Crafting a Legacy

with your life. It's not just about the big achievements—the everyday moments—the kindness you show, the lessons you pass on, and how you make people feel.

What truly matters to you? Is it family? Creativity? Making the world a little better? Write these down. Your values are the compass guiding your legacy. Don't wait to leave a mark. Small actions add up. Hold the door open, mentor someone, or listen when someone needs to talk. Have you ever shared a part of your life with someone and seen how it moved them? Maybe it was a story of triumph, or maybe just a funny moment that brightened their day. Writing, recording, or even sharing your story in conversation ensures your wisdom doesn't fade.

Your legacy doesn't have to be perfect. It's better if it isn't. Let it be confirmed, flawed, and human. Here's the thing: resilience and legacy feed each other. Every hardship you endure shapes your character. And every time you share that strength with others, you add another layer to your legacy.

Imagine that someone who knew you only through your actions wrote your biography. What stories would they tell? Would they recount the times you showed courage when it was easier to give up or when you brought laughter to others, even on difficult days? Legacy isn't built on grand gestures alone. It's in the quiet decisions, the daily efforts to live with integrity, and the small kindnesses that ripple beyond what you can see.

You've probably heard the phrase, "We're all just walking each other home." That's the heart of this chapter. Your resilience isn't just for you—it's a gift to those around you. And your legacy isn't just about the past; it's a light guiding others into the future.

So, take a moment. Reflect on how far you've come. The times you didn't think you'd make it—but you did. Celebrate that. Then think about the legacy you're crafting, whether with grand gestures or quiet kindnesses. You're resilient. You're creating a legacy. And that's something truly extraordinary.

Destructive forces move through life like storms, fierce and unyielding, dismantling what we hold dear. They tear through our lives with unsettling clarity, breaking down illusions, unmasking our vulnerabilities, and leaving us stripped of our essence. Yet, in their wake, they reveal the power of renewal.

Chapter 21: Disintegration & Transformation

Destructive forces are inevitable, but they are also transformative. They challenge us, pushing us to grow in ways we might not have chosen but often need. Understanding these forces—anger, depression, fear, and despair—requires courage and awareness, turning pain into lessons and chaos into clarity.

Anger & Its Roots

Anger is one of the most intense emotions, often emerging when expectations clash with reality. Anger has been a recurring challenge, erupting during criticism or unmet expectations. It's a fiery force that can consume relationships and self-control, yet it also holds the potential for self-awareness and change.

Reflecting on my past, I see how anger often masked more profound vulnerabilities—fear, inadequacy, or a sense of loss. Much of my early anger mirrored patterns I learned from those around me, especially my mother's fiery responses to conflict. Over time, I recognized that anger could destroy or enlighten me, depending on how I handled it.

By examining the roots of anger, I've learned to pause before reacting. Is this feeling rooted in fear? Is it disappointment or unmet needs? This introspection has allowed me to channel anger constructively—whether through creative pursuits, open conversations, or physical activity. Anger, when acknowledged, becomes a catalyst for growth rather than destruction.

Depression: The Silent Companion

Depression often arrives unannounced, like a fog that dims joy and saps energy. It is a deeply personal yet widely shared experience stemming from stress, trauma, or the weight of societal expectations. Unlike anger, which explodes outwardly, depression turns inward, creating a heavy silence that isolates.

For many, depression is compounded by genetic predispositions or family histories, but environment and life experiences also play significant roles. Traumatic events, whether sudden or cumulative, often leave emotional scars that can manifest as depression. Similarly, losing a loved one, a relationship, or a dream—can create a profound sense of emptiness.

21 - Disintegration & Transformation

Interplay of Anger & Depression

Anger and depression are often intertwined. Anger turned inward can manifest as depression, while unresolved depression can fuel outward expressions of anger. Together, they create a cycle that's difficult to break but offers profound insights when understood. Recognizing this connection allows us to approach these emotions with compassion and clarity, transforming them into opportunities for self-awareness.

Healing Process

Healing from anger and depression requires courage. Facing these emotions head-on, rather than avoiding them, helps us uncover their more profound messages. Anger might highlight unmet needs, while depression could signal areas of life out of alignment. By treating these feelings as guides rather than enemies, we begin to heal.

For me, this meant learning to pause and ask, "What is this emotion trying to tell me?" Anger taught me to set boundaries and communicate honestly. Depression, on the other hand, reminded me to seek connection and realign my life with what truly matters.

Transforming Negative to Positive

Destructive emotions can be overwhelming, but they also hold the power for transformation. Anger, for instance, can motivate us to act, while fear can push us out of complacency. By embracing these forces, we can turn obstacles into opportunities for growth. This transformation doesn't mean ignoring negativity but understanding its roots and channeling its energy constructively. Practices like mindfulness, gratitude, and creative expression help reframe our perspectives, turning pain into purpose. We reclaim our power with each step, using life's challenges to build resilience and strength.

Embracing Life's Journey

Animals as Companions

In times of struggle, animals often become lifelines. Their unconditional love and presence offer solace when human connections feel overwhelming or insufficient. My pets—two cats, an aviary of birds, and a Yorkie named Baby—have been constant companions, providing joy, comfort, and grounding.

Animals remind us of the simple pleasures in life: a playful moment, a soft purr, or a wagging tail. Their adaptability teaches resilience, reminding us to face challenges with grace. Caring for them creates a sense of purpose and routine, which can be healing during difficult times.

21 - Disintegration & Transformation

Beyond Destruction

While painful, destructive forces are also pathways to renewal. They challenge us to grow, let go of what no longer serves us, and embrace new possibilities. In navigating life's storms, we cultivate resilience—a legacy not of perfection but of persistence.

Legacy is not just about accomplishments but about the kindness and strength we show in the face of adversity. It's about the love we give, the lessons we share, and the courage we demonstrate. By facing life's challenges gracefully, we create a ripple effect that extends far beyond our individual lives.

Living with Intention

To move beyond destructive forces, we must live intentionally. This means aligning our actions with our values and choosing to see challenges as opportunities for growth. By doing so, we transform pain into purpose, creating a meaningful and fulfilling life.

Destructive forces are not here to break us but to shape us. They push us toward growth, helping us discover strengths we didn't know we had. Through awareness, compassion, and resilience, we navigate these forces, emerging stronger, wiser, and ready to face whatever comes next.

21 - Disintegration & Transformation

Beautiful are those whose brokenness gives birth to transformation and wisdom."

– *John Mark Green*

Embracing Life's Journey

In our final moments of life, memories surge like a tsunami, powerful and consuming. They sweep us into past moments, filling our senses with sights, sounds, and emotions deeply felt once before. They bring both joy and sorrow, carrying fragments of who we were and the lives we once lived.

Chapter 22: Tsunami of Memories

Our brains are remarkable, intricate landscapes that hold the history of our lives. Within this labyrinth of neurons and synapses lie our memories, shaping our identities and grounding us in the present. They are more than recollections; they are the threads that weave the story of who we are. Every memory we hold onto—whether joyous, painful, or mundane—contributes to the narrative of our lives.

Yet, memories are fragile, fleeting, and, in many ways, imperfect. They evolve as we do, colored by emotions and perceptions, often blurring the line between reality and interpretation. This impermanence is both a limitation and a gift. It reminds us of the preciousness of life, urging us to cherish each moment, knowing that it will one day fade into the recesses of our minds.

The Final Surge

As life nears its end, many describe an overwhelming phenomenon: a life review. It's as though a vivid and unrelenting tsunami of memories washes over them. Moments once thought forgotten to resurface with stunning clarity, presenting a mosaic of experiences that encapsulate their lives. This isn't merely a chronological replay—it's an emotional tapestry where the weight of each memory is felt as deeply as the moment it was created.

This surge is more than a biological event; it's a profound reflection of existence. In those moments, the barriers between past and present dissolve, leaving only the essence of what mattered most. We see the love we gave and received, the connections that shaped us, and the lessons learned through triumphs and failures.

The life review is often described as a spiritual experience, a final reckoning with the self. It offers a moment of clarity where life's complexities are distilled into simple truths. In this final crescendo, we are reminded that our lives are not defined by singular achievements or failures but by the totality of our experiences, the relationships we nurtured, and the values we upheld.

The Paradox of Memory and Reality

Our memories are powerful, but they are also subjective. They are shaped by perception, filtered through emotions, and influenced by time. What we remember isn't always an accurate reflection of reality, but it is the reality we carry.

22 - Tsunami of Memories

Einstein once said, "Reality is merely an illusion, albeit very persistent." If our memories define our sense of reality, does this mean we live within constructs of our own making? Are we bound by the narratives we create, or do our memories free us to interpret life in ways that bring meaning and purpose?

The memories that surface during a life review are not random; they are chosen by our subconscious, perhaps as a way to find resolution or closure. In this way, memory serves as a record of the past and a tool for understanding the present and preparing for what lies ahead—even if that future is unknowable.

The Legacy of Memory

The memories we leave behind form the foundation of our legacy. They live on in the hearts and minds of those who knew us, shaping how we are remembered. A legacy isn't solely about monumental achievements; it's about the everyday moments that leave a lasting imprint—the kindness shown, the love shared, the lessons imparted.

When I think about my legacy, it's not the tangible accomplishments I hope will endure but the intangibles: the laughter shared with loved ones, the wisdom passed down, and the courage displayed in times of hardship. These are the memories I hope will ripple through the lives of others, reminding them of the values I held dear.

The Duality of Memories

Memories are both a blessing and a burden. They bring joy and nostalgia but can also carry pain and regret. Yet even painful memories have their place. They teach resilience, empathy, and the importance of forgiveness for others and ourselves.

Memories' duality mirrors life's duality: moments of light balanced by shadows, triumphs tempered by challenges. This balance gives life its richness and depth. To embrace our memories fully, we must accept this duality, recognizing that every experience—joyous or sorrowful—shaped us.

Embracing Life's Journey

Creating New Memories

As long as we live, we can create new memories. Each day is a blank page, waiting to be filled with moments that will one day form the chapters of our life story. This perspective encourages us to be present, to savor the small joys, and to approach life with gratitude.

One of the most profound ways to create meaningful memories is through connection. Whether spending time with loved ones, sharing stories, or simply being present, these interactions form the foundation of our most cherished recollections.

Navigating the Tsunami

The tsunami of memories can feel overwhelming, especially when they resurface unexpectedly. But they also offer an opportunity for growth and healing. By revisiting our memories with compassion and curiosity, we can find meaning in our experiences and integrate them into the broader narrative of our lives.

22 - Tsunami of Memories 174

When memories resurface, ask yourself: What is this memory trying to teach me? How has it shaped who I am today? By reflecting on these questions, we can transform painful memories into sources of wisdom and strength.

A Final Reflection

As we navigate the ebb and flow of life, let us strive to create memories that fill us with pride and gratitude. Let us cherish the present moment, knowing it will one day become a memory. And let us remember that, in the end, our lives are not defined by the memories we hold but by the love and impact we leave behind.

In the final surge of memories, when the tsunami comes crashing down, may we find peace knowing we lived fully, loved deeply, and embraced the journey with all its joys and challenges.

Embracing Life's Journey

Embracing life as an ever-evolving story not bound by finality means letting go of rigid conclusions, staying open to change, and leaving room for new colors on life's canvas.

Chapter 23: Unfinishing Your Life

We often seek closure and tidy endings in our quest for a meaningful life. Yet, life itself resists such simplicity. Rather than a series of completed stories, life is more like an evolving landscape—open-ended, with unanswered questions and unexpected turns. To truly embrace this reality, we can let go of the need for finality and instead focus on the joy of discovery, finding meaning in the process of "unfinishing."

As we age and reflect, many of us find ourselves considering the paths we didn't take, the dreams left unfulfilled, and the relationships that ended before resolving. Initially, these loose threads may seem like missed opportunities, but what if they're integral to a life fully lived? Perhaps a meaningful life is less about tying up every loose end and more about embracing the questions and experiences that remain open, allowing them to enrich our journey in ways that a rigid focus on closure could never achieve.

Beauty of an Unfinished Life

The concept of "unfinished" often conveys incompleteness or lack of accomplishment. However, there is a distinct beauty in allowing ourselves to be works in progress. We're not novels with a fixed ending;

rather, we're like ever-evolving poems, constantly adding verses, each blending into the next. Every day offers a chance to grow, shift, and add a new dimension to who we are, regardless of what's left undone.

To capture this richness, many people create bucket lists—a life map filled with aspirations, dreams, and goals. Unlike a checklist, however, a bucket list is more of a manifesto, reflecting our desire to experience life fully. Each item is an acknowledgment of life's abundance and potential. Writing down these dreams brings them closer to reality, whether it's visiting a far-off country, learning a new skill, or deepening a relationship. Ironically, the more we achieve, the more new dreams emerge. This constant expansion embodies the essence of an unfinished life, where growth and desire perpetually inspire us to keep moving forward.

Unfinished Dreams

Accepting that not every bucket list item will be checked off is liberating. Rather than seeing an incomplete list as a failure, we can view it as a testament to an engaged, ever-curious spirit. Unfinished dreams remind us of life's finite nature, inviting us to savor each moment and step. An incomplete list is a portrait of resilience—a reminder of our relentless curiosity and engagement with the world. By releasing the pressure to "finish," we can find satisfaction in the journey itself.

An unfinished life is one lived with openness to change. It encourages us to embrace uncertainty and explore new paths without feeling bound to a single destination. Rather than holding onto rigid plans or aspirations, we can learn to accept that some dreams will remain just that—dreams. Far from diminishing their worth, this perspective honors that each aspiration has contributed to our growth and added depth to our journey, whether realized or not.

Meaning Beyond Completion

The search for meaning doesn't require a tidy ending. Life's true significance is often found not in our accomplishments but in the richness of our experiences and relationships. Our lives don't need definitive endings to be fulfilling; by embracing life as a series of open doors, we can focus more on the connections we make and the lessons we learn. Living an unfinished life isn't about abandoning dreams; it's about holding them lightly, allowing ourselves to be present with what each moment brings, rather than rushing toward a final goal.

Unfinished dreams and ambitions can serve as reminders of our deeper values. These open aspirations can ground us in the present, providing a sense of continuity without pressuring us to reach a fixed endpoint. As we move through life, we often find that what we once considered essential may shift, allowing space for new values and goals to emerge. This adaptability is one of the most powerful aspects of a well-lived life.

Art of Living in the Unknown

Stepping into the unknown can be intimidating. Many of us cling to familiar routines and identities as sources of comfort, even if they no longer serve us. True growth, however, requires a willingness to venture beyond what is familiar, trusting that we will find strength in exploration. In reflecting on my life, I see how staying too long in certain relationships or situations limits my potential for transformation. Embracing change means stepping away from comfort and welcoming the unknown, which, though challenging, is often where we find our greatest growth.

Living an unfinished life means valuing the present over the future and trusting that life itself is meaningful, whether or not we achieve everything we set out to do. It's about engaging with each day as it comes, taking risks, and remaining curious, all while accepting that we may never have all the answers.

Legacy in the Unfinished

Our legacy, too, is part of this unfolding journey. We often think of legacy as concrete—a body of work, a finished product, or a final accomplishment. However, a legacy built on an unfinished life is not only about what we leave behind but also our ongoing influence on others through our actions, words, and the values we embody. Our legacy may be found in the memories we create with loved ones, the kindness we offer to strangers, or the inspiration we give others to continue their journeys of exploration.

23 - Unfinishing Your Life

An unfinished legacy reflects our openness to life's ongoing questions, signaling that our value lies not in the accolades we collect but in the lives we touch. By embracing life's inherent uncertainty, we model resilience and curiosity, offering a legacy of love, connection, and encouragement for those we leave behind.

Open-Ended Story

To live an unfinished life is to fully embrace each day with curiosity and a willingness to evolve. It's about recognizing that life is a story without a definitive ending, one in which each chapter brings new lessons, challenges, and joys. When we approach life as an open-ended journey, we free ourselves from the pressure to complete every goal and can instead savor each experience for what it is. Life becomes less about achieving a final state of perfection and more about engaging with each chapter and scene as it unfolds.

The truth is the journey of life will always be in motion. We are constantly growing, adapting, and facing new challenges. There is no final state of "having it all figured out"—the beauty of life lies in its unfolding, the balance of joy and struggle, and the lessons we gather along the way. Embracing the notion of "unfinishing" allows us to experience life's richness without concluding.

Celebrating Life's Incompleteness

An unfinished life is an ongoing symphony that values process over finality. It teaches us to live with an open heart and mind, understanding that we don't need to achieve everything to lead a meaningful life. In these final chapters, we've explored ideas like resilience, acceptance, humor, and wisdom. But the most significant lesson is that life isn't a race to the finish—it's about fully inhabiting each moment, learning to let go, and finding joy in laughter and tears.

This perspective doesn't negate the importance of goals or dreams; instead, it helps us pursue them with a spirit of openness and curiosity, knowing that the journey is where life's meaning is found. By letting go of the need for completion, we make room for wonder, growth, and the unfolding of a life lived fully.

Gift of an Unfinished Life

I hope you'll be open to the unknown as you close this book. Embrace life's unpredictability, meet challenges with resilience, and find humor in its absurdities. Wisdom lies not in perfection but in the richness of experience. The greatest gift we can give ourselves is to live with curiosity, kindness, and the understanding that we are always growing.

In the end, to live an unfinished life is to live deeply, to savor the moments, and to trust that each step, whether forward or backward, holds value. Your journey doesn't end here; it's just the beginning. Know that your path is meaningful, even if it's winding. Embrace the beauty of an unfinished life, and remember that the journey, not the destination, makes life worth living.

23 - Unfinishing Your Life

"For a long time, it had seemed to me that life was about to begin—real life. But there was always some obstacle in the way, something to be gotten through first, some unfinished business, time still to be served, a debt to be paid. Then life would begin. At last, it dawned on me that these obstacles *were* my life."

– *James Patterson*

Find a quiet place and appropriate time to reflect on and realign with your core principles or those shared throughout this book. Embrace them as a source of strength, grounding yourself in gratitude, growth, and resilience.

Chapter 24: An Affirmation of Purpose

Dual Power of Meditation & Affirmation

To lead a life guided by purpose, we must embrace meditation and affirmation—two practices that complement each other profoundly. While meditation soothes the wounds of life, offering healing and restoration, affirmation provides a compass for moving forward, empowering us to live with intention and clarity. Together, they create a balanced approach to navigating life's complexities, allowing us to embrace our journey with resilience, hope, and gratitude.

Why Meditation Matters

Life's challenges often leave emotional, mental, or even physical scars. Meditation addresses these scars with care and intention, ensuring they do not hinder our growth or dim our light. It's about tending to ourselves holistically, recognizing that healing is not a passive process but an active commitment to self-care and renewal.

Meditation isn't just about addressing physical ailments—it's soothing the soul. Whether through mindfulness, therapy, connecting with nature, or seeking support from loved ones, meditation is a way to acknowledge our pain and take steps to heal. It reminds us that it's okay to pause, to nurture ourselves, and to seek help when needed.

At its core, meditation is an act of self-compassion. It's the willingness to care for ourselves as we would for a dear friend, offering kindness rather than judgment. By meditating on our emotional wounds—whether they stem from loss, failure, or fear—we create space for renewal. This process allows us to carry the lessons of the past without being weighed down by its burdens.

The Role of Affirmation

If meditation heals the wounds of the past, affirmation shapes future possibilities. Affirmation is the practice of declaring our values, intentions, and purpose with conviction. It is a way of aligning ourselves with what truly matters, creating a mental framework that supports growth and positivity.

Affirmations are not empty words; they are commitments to ourselves. They help us clarify our vision, bolster our confidence, and keep us grounded when life feels overwhelming. By regularly affirming our purpose, we reinforce the narrative that we are capable, resilient, and deserving of a life aligned with our values.

For example, affirming "I am enough" can counter feelings of inadequacy, while "I trust in my ability to overcome challenges" provides strength during difficult times. These statements may seem simple, but they carry the power to rewire our thoughts, replacing self-doubt with self-belief.

The Interplay of Meditation & Affirmation

Meditation and affirmation are not opposing forces but two sides of the same coin. Meditation addresses the pain of the past, while affirmation builds the foundation for a brighter future. Together, they help us navigate life's highs and lows with grace and strength. Consider a tree tending to its roots, ensuring it has the nourishment it needs to stand tall. Affirmation is the sunlight encouraging the tree's growth. Metaphorically, the roots weaken without meditation, and the tree cannot thrive. Without affirmation, the tree stagnates, unable to reach its full potential.

This dynamic balance is essential for living a life of purpose. Meditation ensures we don't carry unresolved pain into the future, while affirmation helps us stay aligned with our values and aspirations.

Together, they create a cycle of healing and growth that allows us to move forward with resilience and clarity.

Affirmation of Purpose

To anchor these ideas, here is an affirmation designed to inspire and guide:

I am guided by purpose.

With each step, I embrace the opportunity to grow.

I see life as a symphony—a blend of chaos and harmony—where each high and low note enriches the melody of my journey.

I welcome the beauty in the unknown and transform challenges into opportunities with grace.

I honor time and space as forces shaping my unique path, knowing they flow through and around me.

My experiences build resilience, deepen my empathy, and cultivate wisdom.

I accept that insight unfolds gradually, shaped by both light and shadow.

I recognize life's contrasts—joy and pain, love and loss—as essential to my personal growth.

24 - An Affirmation of Purpose

I embrace challenges as a teacher, refining my spirit and broadening my understanding.

I seek balance, trust my intuition, and choose empathy over judgment, allowing each choice to guide me toward my true self.

I remain attuned to my senses, aware of the world's subtle messages, drawing me deeper into the present.

I find meaning in triumphs and struggles, releasing fear and embracing love.

As I move forward, I cultivate the power of positive vision, trusting the unknown and welcoming change.

I flow with life's constant shifts, curious and grateful for this miraculous journey.

In peace and gratitude, I honor each step, each lesson, and every opportunity for growth.

Transformative Power

By integrating meditation and affirmation into our lives, we empower ourselves to face life's challenges with strength and hope. We acknowledge the wounds of the past without letting them define us, and we create a vision for the future rooted in our deepest values. This way, we transform our relationship with ourselves and the world around us. We become agents of positivity, spreading hope and resilience through our words, actions, and presence.

As you reflect on this chapter, consider how to incorporate these practices into your life. What wounds need your care? What affirmations resonate with your purpose? Committing to these practices takes a decisive step toward living a life of meaning, balance, and fulfillment.

In healing and affirming, we embrace the full spectrum of life, honoring its challenges while celebrating its possibilities. Together, these practices form the foundation for a life well-lived, guiding us toward our highest potential with grace and gratitude.

Columbo, the character played by Peter Falk in the classic TV series, isn't typically known for delivering lofty philosophical quotes. Instead, his wisdom is embedded in his unassuming and down-to-earth demeanor, often delivered through his observations of human behavior, such as: "You know, sir, people don't usually think of themselves as bad. They have to find a reason for what they do, even if it's not a good one."

Chapter 25: Just One More Thing

There's something timeless about the way Peter Falk portrayed Detective Columbo. He had that endearing way of turning back when the suspect thought they were off the hook. With his wrinkled trench coat and unassuming demeanor, Columbo would say, "Just one more thing," catching the guilty party off guard with the question that would unravel it all.

That phrase, "Just one more thing," perfectly captures how I feel at the end of this book. As I reach the final pages, there's still a lingering thought, an echo of something left unsaid. After pouring my heart into this journey, I can't help but feel there's one last insight to share.

Embracing Life's Journey

Reflecting on writing this book, I realize that, in many ways, it's been like Columbo's investigations—asking questions, circling back, uncovering truths not noticed at first glance. Life, after all, is a series of discoveries, and as soon as we think we've got it all figured out, there's always just one more thing.

Growing Up in a Different World

The world I grew up in was vastly different from today. I was a young boy in the 1950s—a time of innocence, where doors were left unlocked, and neighbors knew one another by name. It was a time of post-war optimism when families gathered around the radio and television as we watched America dream bigger than ever before.

25 - Just One More Thing

Then came the 1960s, and I was a teenager, filled with all that era's energy, rebellion, and curiosity. The world was changing, and so was I. The civil rights movement, the Beatles, the moon landing—it felt like anything was possible. This vibrant, almost electric, sense of hope was in the air. We were questioning everything, pushing boundaries, and exploring new ways of thinking.

The 1970s brought me to New York City, where I chased my dream of becoming an actor. I studied at the American Academy of Dramatic Arts, immersing myself in theater and performance. Living in a city that never sleeps was a time of self-discovery. I remember feeling like I was part of something larger than myself, surrounded by the arts, the lights, and the energy of a place where dreams could come true.

I used to think 2000 was the future, a distant, almost mythical time.

Embracing Life's Journey

When Stanley Kubrick's 2001: A Space Odyssey was released, it seemed like we were on the cusp of something extraordinary. I watched as the world transformed, as technology brought us closer and made us more distant. The speed at which things change can be dizzying, yet, here we are, navigating it all with the same human spirit that has carried us through centuries.

A Life of Gratitude & Reflection

I've been incredibly fortunate in my journey, and I recognize that. I've had a wonderful life filled with rich experiences, challenges, and moments of sheer joy. Much of that I owe to my mother, Shirley-Mae Schneider. She instilled in me confidence, creativity, and a sense of playfulness.

25 - Just One More Thing

For the last decade, I have been her caretaker, sharing precious moments, laughter, and the deep connection that only comes from genuinely being there for someone. She passed away in 2024, the same year this book was published. Though this book is dedicated to my daughter, my mother's spirit is woven into every page. Her memory is the guiding light that continues to inspire me.

I've dedicated the rest of my life to honoring her legacy—by living with the creativity, kindness, and resilience she taught me, finding joy in the small things, never taking myself too seriously, and embracing each new day as a chance to grow, learn, and give back.

The Final Lesson

Writing this book taught me that life is not about perfection, having all the answers, or reaching a state of unshakeable wisdom. It's about embracing the questions, staying curious, and being open to the unexpected. If only we could take the time to look, the world would be full of wonder.

The ongoing search for meaning is the beauty of it all. Life isn't something to be solved or perfected; it's something to be experienced, with all its messiness and surprises.

Like some of Columbo's cases, life's questions are never fully answered. It is in the asking, however, that we uncover life's beauty. So? What questions will you explore?

25 - Just One More Thing

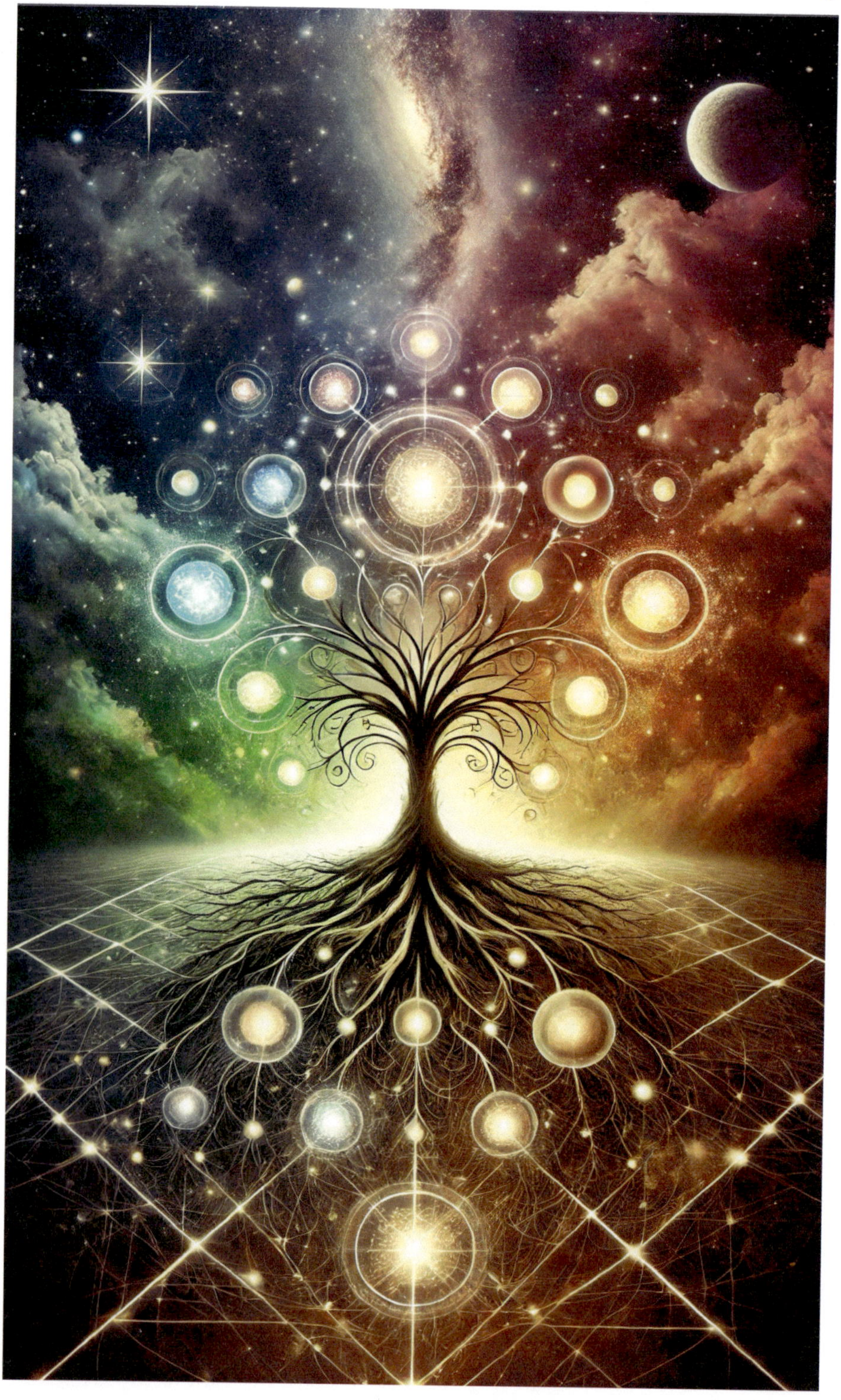

Glossary of Concepts & Terms (Alphabetical Order)

Affirmation of Purpose — A powerful reflection to realign oneself with core values, grounding in gratitude, resilience, and continuous growth.

Artificial Intelligence (AI) — Computer-driven systems that perform tasks requiring human intelligence, such as learning, problem-solving, and language processing. It includes machine learning, where algorithms improve with data and natural language processing.

Artificial Stimulants — Substances like drugs or alcohol that alter sensory and emotional experiences. Overreliance can disrupt emotional balance and long-term well-being.

Balance of Rational and Intuitive Thought — The integration of logic and instinct in decision-making. Emphasizes harmony between intellect and intuition for effective choices.

Birth as a Symphony — A metaphor likening the beginning of life to a symphony, blending the chaos and rhythm of birth with the harmony of existence.

Cyclical Nature of Life — Life's cycles of birth, growth, decay, and renewal. Emphasizes the importance of embracing endings as precursors to new beginnings.

Chaos Theory — Suggests that small changes in complex systems can have far-reaching consequences, illustrating life's randomness and interconnectedness.

Cycles of Renewal — Embracing natural disintegration as part of life's transformative process. Every end is also a beginning, renewing life's energy.

Embracing Life's Journey — Fully engaging with life's phases—its challenges, triumphs, and uncertainties. Encourages valuing experiences, relationships, and personal growth over fixed goals.

Emotional Perception — The skill of interpreting emotions, connecting empathy and intuition, and fostering meaningful human connections.

Existential Thought — A philosophical approach to understanding life's unpredictability, emphasizing creating personal meaning through choices and relationships.

Fate vs. Randomness — The balance between destiny and chance in shaping life challenges us to consider how much control we truly have.

Fluidity of Identity — The evolving nature of personal and collective identity demonstrates how experiences reshape who we are.

Inner Dialogue — The ongoing internal conversation of various voices (experience, fear, hope, and wisdom). Managing this dialogue is vital for self-awareness and growth.

Intuitive Rationalization — Making decisions based on gut feelings, later justified through logic. Highlights the role of intuition in guiding actions.

Judging, Evaluating, and Measuring — Excessive judgment and comparison drain energy. Emphasizes focusing on meaningful pursuits rather than superficial assessments.

Legacy in the Unfinished — Viewing legacy not as a completed project but as an ongoing influence through everyday actions and values.

Metaphysics of Transformation — The philosophical exploration of change and evolution, both physical and spiritual.

Metaphor — A figure of speech comparing two things to highlight shared qualities, making abstract concepts more relatable.

Paradox and Irony — Paradoxes reveal deeper truths by challenging our understanding, while irony contrasts expectations with reality.

Positively Remembering Pain — Reframing past traumas to build resilience, empathy, and wisdom.

Glossary of Concepts & Terms

Sensory Overstimulation — The modern challenge of constant sensory exposure leading to disconnection. Mindfulness reconnects us with more profound experiences.

Spiritual Awareness — Embracing intangible aspects of life, fostering interconnectedness and meaning beyond the physical.

Stimulating Senses — Sensory experiences shape awareness and connection to the world. They encourage mindfulness to appreciate life's subtleties.

Symphony of Life — A metaphor comparing life to a symphony, illustrating the interplay of chaos, order, and beauty.

Time & Space Conundrum — Inspired by Einstein's theory of relativity, this chapter explores how time and space shape human experience and transformation.

Transformative Nature of Pain — The idea that pain acts as a catalyst for growth, fostering resilience and deeper understanding.

Visualization and Positive Thinking — Using mental imagery and positivity to shape reality, transforming intentions into actions.

Voice of Experience — The inner guidance that develops with age, balancing optimism and caution for sound decision-making.

Voice of Negativity — Represents doubt and caution, protecting against risks but potentially causing anxiety if overemphasized.

Voice of Positivity — The internal advocate for hope and optimism, encouraging risk-taking and a positive outlook on life.

Wisdom as a Miracle — Wisdom goes beyond knowledge, emerging unexpectedly from life's challenges, blending rationality with intuition.

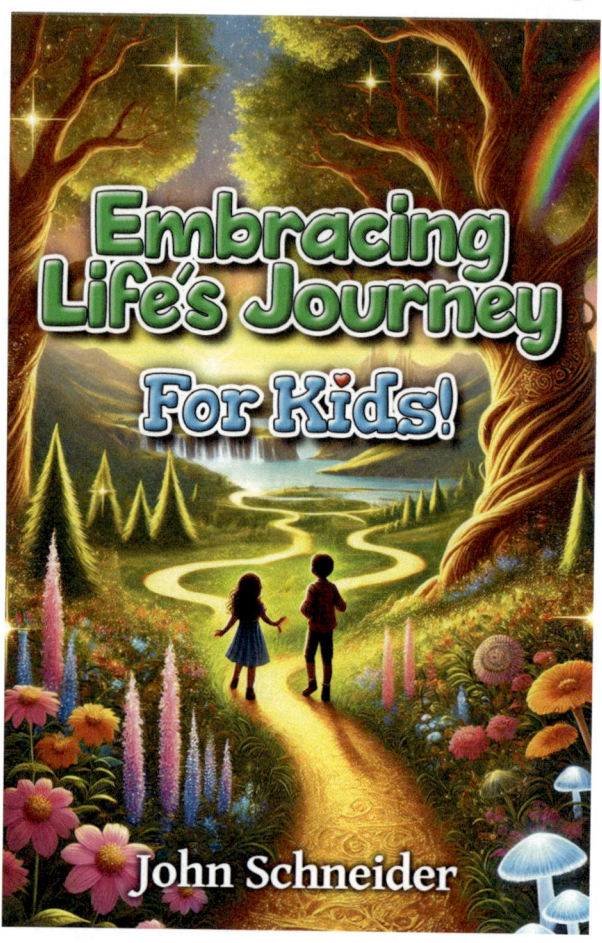

Embracing Life's Journey for Kids is a children's book designed to inspire mindfulness, resilience, and self-discovery through engaging stories and simple activities. The book helps children navigate their emotions, build confidence, and embrace the world with curiosity and kindness. Perfect for ages 5-10, this book offers valuable lessons in calmness, courage, and gratitude, encouraging kids to uncover their unique strengths and enjoy life's little moments.

Bibliography & Suggested Reading

A Brief History of Everything (Shambhala Publications, 1996) by Ken Wilber—Wilber provides a comprehensive exploration of consciousness and personal growth, synthesizing Eastern and Western philosophies.

A Brief History of Time (Bantam Books, 1988) by Stephen Hawking—This groundbreaking work explores complex scientific concepts like time, black holes, and the universe's nature, delving into existential questions about origins, our place within it, and the quest for understanding.

A Historical Journey Across Raritan Bay (Arcadia History Press, 2018) by John Schneider—Schneider provides a rich historical account of Raritan Bay, exploring the cultural, social, and geographical factors shaping its communities.

A Year to Live—How to Live This Year as If It Were Your Last (Harmony Books, 1997) by Stephen Levine—Levine proposes living with the mindset of having one year left, offering practical exercises for cultivating compassion and mindfulness.

Atomic Habits (Penguin Random House, 2018) by James Clear—Offers a proven framework for building good habits and breaking bad ones, emphasizing small, consistent changes for significant improvement.

Brief Answers to the Big Questions (Bantam Books, 2018) by Stephen Hawking—Hawking's final book addresses questions about humanity's future, artificial intelligence, and the existence of God, exploring purpose, scientific curiosity, and human potential.

Care of the Soul—A Guide for Cultivating Depth and Sacredness in Everyday Life (HarperCollins, 1992) by Thomas Moore—Moore offers a philosophical approach to nurturing the soul, blending psychology with spiritual principles for inner peace and fulfillment.

Daring Greatly: How the Courage to Be Vulnerable Transforms the Way We Live, Love, Parent, and Lead (Gotham Books, 2012) by Brené Brown—Brown discusses vulnerability as a source of strength, encouraging openness and authenticity based on years of research.

Emotional Intelligence—Why It Can Matter More Than IQ (Bantam Books, 1995) by Daniel Goleman—This influential book introduces emotional intelligence (EQ) and its importance for personal and professional success, emphasizing self-awareness and empathy.

Flourish—A Visionary New Understanding of Happiness and Well-being (Free Press, 2011) by Martin E.P. Seligman—Expanding on positive psychology research, Seligman introduces the PERMA model (Positive emotion, Engagement, Relationships, Meaning, and Achievement).

Flow—The Psychology of Optimal Experience (Harper & Row, 1990) by Mihaly Csikszentmihalyi—Explores "flow," a state of immersion where individuals feel highly focused and energized, linking it to greater happiness and productivity.

Immunity to Change—How to Overcome It and Unlock the Potential in Yourself and Your Organization (Harvard Business Press, 2009) by Robert Kegan and Lisa Laskow Lahey—Explores psychological barriers to growth, offering a framework to recognize and dismantle obstacles in personal and professional realms.

Incognito—The Secret Lives of the Brain (Pantheon Books, 2011) by David Eagleman—Eagleman delves into neuroscience, explaining the hidden processes behind human thought and behavior, making complex ideas accessible.

Man's Search for Meaning (Beacon Press, 1959) by Viktor E. Frankl—Frankl recounts his experiences in concentration camps, introducing logotherapy and exploring purpose in suffering as a core element of resilience.

Mindset—The New Psychology of Success (Random House, 2006) by Carol S. Dweck—Dweck introduces "fixed" and "growth" mindsets, explaining how beliefs about abilities shape behavior and success and advocating for resilience.

Outliers—The Story of Success (Little, Brown and Company, 2008) by Malcolm Gladwell—Gladwell investigates hidden factors behind high achievement, examining how culture, timing, and practice contribute to success.

Self-Determination Theory—Basic Psychological Needs in Motivation, Development, and Wellness (Guilford Press, 2017) by

Bibliography & Suggested Reading

Richard M. Ryan and Edward L. Deci—The authors present a theory on intrinsic motivation, emphasizing autonomy, competence, and relatedness in personal growth.

Shambhala—The Sacred Path of the Warrior (Shambhala Publications, 1984) by Chögyam Trungpa—This guide blends Eastern wisdom and practical advice for cultivating courage, compassion, and resilience.

Soul Seeker: Reflections on a Spiritual Journey from Darkness to the Light by Michael T. Houghton (aka Perspectus) shares reflections on a true story from constant pain and suicidal thoughts to healing, redemption, and spirituality. The author's reflections shared through his prose, poetry, and photography, begin with him being trapped in a deep depression resulting from a five-year battle with constant pain from an autoimmune disorder. Feeling hopeless and powerless, he hits the "darkest night of his soul" and decides to end his life. But this book is not about suicide, but rather redemption.

The 7 Habits of Highly Effective People: Powerful Lessons in Personal Change (Free Press, 1989) by Stephen R. Covey—A classic self-help book presenting seven principles for personal and professional effectiveness through proactive behaviors and prioritizing.

The Art of Living—Peace and Freedom in the Here and Now (Harper One, 2017) by Thich Nhat Hanh—Nhat Hanh shares Buddhist wisdom for mindfulness, encouraging presence, compassion, and understanding life's impermanence.

The Power of Now—A Guide to Spiritual Enlightenment (New World Library, 1997) by Eckhart Tolle—Tolle explains how living in the present moment leads to spiritual awakening, inner peace, and a reduction in stress.

The Prophet (Knopf, 1923) by Kahlil Gibran—Gibran's poetic work explores universal themes of love, freedom, and self-knowledge through the reflections of a prophet leaving his homeland, offering philosophical and spiritual insights.

The Road to Character (Random House, 2015) by David Brooks—Brooks contrasts external achievements with inner virtues, emphasizing humility, moral development, and integrity through the lives of historical figures.

The Subtle Art of Not Giving a F*ck (HarperOne, 2016) by Mark Manson—Challenges conventional self-help advice, advocating for embracing life's challenges and focusing on what truly matters.

The Universe in a Nutshell (Bantam Books, 2001) by Stephen Hawking builds on concepts from A Brief History of Time, expanding on relativity, quantum mechanics, and the universe's structure. It encourages readers to question their perceptions and understanding.

The Varieties of Religious Experience—A Study in Human Nature (Longmans, Green, and Co., 1902) by William James—A classic examination of the psychological aspects of religious experiences, discussing spirituality's influence on human life.

Toward a Psychology of Being (Van Nostrand, 1962) by Abraham H. Maslow—Maslow presents his theory of self-actualization, exploring human potential and the drive for personal growth.

When Things Fall Apart: Heart Advice for Difficult Times (Shambhala Publications, 1997) by Pema Chodron—Chodron offers insights on facing life's challenges with compassion and mindfulness, transforming difficulty into personal growth.

Wherever You Go, There You Are: Mindfulness Meditation in Everyday Life (Hyperion, 1994) by Jon Kabat-Zinn—Kabat-Zinn introduces mindfulness practices to reduce stress, increase focus, and cultivate peace.

Who Moved My Cheese? An A-Mazing Way to Deal with Change in Your Work and in Your Life (Putnam Adult, 1998) by Spencer Johnson—A simple allegory about adaptability and resilience, encouraging readers to embrace change to navigate life's uncertainties.

Willpower: Rediscovering the Greatest Human Strength (Penguin Press, 2011) by Roy F. Baumeister and John Tierney—Explores the science of self-control, examining how willpower works, its limitations, and strategies for improving it, with insights from psychology and neuroscience.

You Are a Badass (Running Press, 2013) by Jen Sincero—Provides stories, exercises, and advice on identifying and changing self-sabotaging behavior, overcoming fears, and finding self-love.

About the Author

Born 1949 in Fort Lauderdale, FL, John Schneider embodies the spirit of a true Renaissance man. His journey from the sun-soaked streets of Florida to the vibrant heart of New Jersey reflects a life filled with exploration, creativity, and unwavering curiosity. Over the years, John has woven a rich tapestry of accomplishments across diverse fields, delving into journalism, geophysics, broadcasting, marketing, and historical research. Each of these experiences contributes to the depth and breadth of his writing.

John's academic path began with a degree in journalism and geophysics from the University of Maryland, where his love for analytical thinking and storytelling took root. This foundation paved the way for a career that spanned radio broadcasting, television hosting, and an executive role as Vice President of Marketing at AT&T. His extensive communication experience allowed him to connect with audiences on multiple levels, transforming complex ideas into engaging narratives.

Recognized as one of the top fifty historians of the past fifty years in Monmouth County, NJ, John has dedicated much of his life to preserving and sharing the stories of the region he calls home. His works, such as A Historical Journey Across Raritan Bay and Sandy Hook, New Jersey—Past & Present, are beloved for their vivid portrayal of local heritage. For readers interested in exploring these historical works further, visit AHistoricalJourney.com.

John's relentless intellectual curiosity drives him to question the ordinary and explore the extraordinary. His passion for new ideas and understanding the randomness of life's journey is a testament to his belief that "life's beauty is found in its contradictions—the intelligence hidden within chaos, the wisdom that emerges from uncertainty."

Raising his daughter Jeanne while navigating personal hardships like divorce has deepened his empathy and understanding of life's complexities. These experiences enrich his perspective, adding authenticity to the themes explored in Embracing Life's Journey. His ongoing creative ventures include producing New Jersey Bayshore Living, a 30-minute weekly television program on Comcast, and leading his media company, CreateAVision Media. In addition to his literary achievements, John is also an accomplished visual artist, musician, and songwriter, embodying the philosophy that life is an endless journey of learning and self-discovery.

Through his writing, John Schneider invites readers to reflect on their lives with curiosity, resilience, and an open heart. His ability to draw from many personal experiences, professional insights, and philosophical musings offers readers a thoughtful, well-rounded approach to navigating life's challenges. His work guides readers to embrace life with creativity, humility, and a touch of humor, encouraging us all to find grace in the journey.

Made in the USA
Columbia, SC
11 April 2025